P9-DDL-681

ISSUES and ANSWERS in JESUS' DAY

BIBLE STUDY GUIDE

From the Bible-teaching ministry of

Charles R. Swindoll

INSIGHT FOR LIVING

Charles R. Swindoll is a graduate of Dallas Theological Seminary and has served in pastorates in Texas, Massachusetts, and California since 1963. He has served as senior pastor of the First Evangelical Free Church of Fullerton, California, since 1971. Chuck's radio program, "Insight for Living," began in 1979. In addition to his church and radio ministries, Chuck enjoys writing. He has authored numerous books and booklets on a variety of subjects.

Based on the outlines and transcripts of Chuck's sermons, the study guide text is coauthored by Ken Gire, a graduate of Texas Christian University and Dallas Theological Seminary. The Living Insights are also written by Ken Gire.

Editor in Chief:
Cynthia Swindoll

Coauthor of Text:
Ken Gire

Assistant Editor:
Glenda Schlahta

Copy Manager:
Jac La Tour

Copyediting Supervisor:
Marty Anderson

Copy Editor:
Wendy Peterson

Art Director:
Steven Mitchell

Designer:
Gary Lett

Production Artists:
Gary Lett and Diana Vasquez

Typesetter:
Bob Haskins

Director, Communications Division:
Carla Beck

Project Manager:
Alene Cooper

Print Production Manager:
Deedee Snyder

Assistant Production Manager:
John Norton

Printer:
Frye and Smith

Unless otherwise identified, all Scripture references are from the New American Standard Bible, © The Lockman Foundation 1960, 1962, 1963, 1968, 1971, 1972, 1973, 1975, 1977. Used by permission.

An effort has been made to locate sources and obtain permission where necessary for the quotations used in this book. In the event of any unintentional omission, a modification will gladly be incorporated in future printings.

ISBN 0-8499-8413-0
Printed in the United States of America.

COVER PAINTING: *Ecce Homo* ("Behold the Man"), by Antonio Ciseri. From the Galleria d'Arte Moderna, Firenze, Italy, Scala/Art Resource. The title of this painting comes from John 19:5. Pilate, having found no guilt in Jesus, nevertheless had Him scourged to pacify the crowd. After the scourging—where the soldiers also beat Him, mocked Him, and put the crown of thorns on His head—Pilate offered Jesus to the crowd once again. They shouted, "Crucify Him!"

CONTENTS

* This message was not a part of the original series but is compatible with it.

INTRODUCTION

Many people have a strange idea that the issues people wrestled with in Jesus' day were quite different from the ones we face today. This misconception leads them to believe that the Bible is somewhat out of touch and irrelevant . . . including even the teachings of Jesus.

When I did my original work on the material that appears in this study guide, I was overwhelmed with the evidence that proves otherwise. Again and again I found that the questions our Lord asked and answered, as well as the issues He addressed, were right on target with many of the things people struggle with today.

My hope is that this study will accomplish two objectives: make all of us aware of how timely Scripture really is and reinforce our confidence in Christ's counsel. The questions He asks are relevant. The answers He provides are right. I am convinced of this, without reservation. Hopefully, all who study these chapters soon will be too.

Chuck Swindoll

PUTTING TRUTH
INTO ACTION

Knowledge apart from application falls short of God's desire for His children. He wants us to apply what we learn so that we will change and grow. This study guide was prepared with these goals in mind. As you go through the following pages, we hope your desire to discover biblical truth will grow as your understanding of God's Word increases, and that you will be encouraged to apply what you've learned.

To assist you in your study, we've included a section called Living Insights at the end of each lesson. These exercises will challenge you to study further and to think of specific ways to put your discoveries into action.

There are many ways to use this guide—in personal devotions, group studies, discussions with friends and family, and Sunday school classes. And, of course, it's an ideal study aid when you're listening to its corresponding "Insight for Living" radio series.

To benefit most from this study guide, we would encourage you to consider it a spiritual journal. That's why we've included space in the Living Insights for recording your thoughts and discoveries. We hope you'll return to those sections often for review and encouragement as you continue to grow in your walk with Christ.

Ken Gire

Ken Gire
Coauthor of Text
Author of Living Insights

ISSUES and ANSWERS in JESUS' DAY

Chapter 1

WHO DO PEOPLE SAY THE SON OF MAN IS?

Matthew 16:13–17

The identity of Jesus is like a jigsaw puzzle, which has been placed in each person's hands to piece together before coming to some kind of conclusion. Leaders from Pontius Pilate to the President of the United States have worked to fit the fragments of His life into an intelligible composite. Many who have labored over His enigmatic claims have stood up and walked away from that puzzle in rejection. Still others have successfully put the pieces together and have sunk to their knees in worship. One such leader, surprisingly, was Napoleon Bonaparte.

> I know man, and I tell you that Jesus is not a man! The religion of Christ is a mystery which subsists by its own force, and proceeds from a mind which is not a human mind. We find in it a marked individuality, which originated a train of words and maxims unknown before. Jesus borrowed nothing from our knowledge. He exhibited in himself the perfect example of his precepts. Jesus is not a philosopher; for his proofs are miracles, and from the first his disciples adored him. In fact, learning and philosophy are of no use for salvation; and Jesus came into the world to reveal the mysteries of heaven and the laws of the Spirit.
>
> Alexander, Caesar, Charlemagne and myself founded empires; but upon what did we rest the creations of our genius? Upon *force*. Jesus Christ alone founded his empire upon love; and at this hour millions of men would die for him.[1]

1. Napoleon Bonaparte, as quoted in *Behold the Man: An Anthology of Jesus Christ*, ed. Ralph L. Woods (New York, N.Y.: Macmillan Co., 1944), pp. 123–24.

Jesus. Such a remarkable man—one who has captured the hearts of shepherds and kings, of tax collectors and artists, of thieves and religious teachers, of prostitutes and philosophers—warrants our scrutiny.

That thought is the impetus for this series, which centers on questions Jesus asked, as well as questions His contemporaries asked about Him. In this opening lesson, we want to ask and answer a question Jesus put to His disciples: "Who do people say that the Son of Man is?"

A Few Introductory Remarks about Questions

In his book *Night*, set during the World War II Nazi persecution of the Jews, Elie Wiesel records a favorite saying of his religious mentor, Moshe the Beadle: "Man raises himself toward God by the questions he asks Him."[2]

From John the Baptist's inquiry, "Are You the [Messiah], or shall we look for someone else?" (Matt. 11:3), to the Pharisees' interrogation, "Who can forgive sins but God alone?" (Mark 2:7), questions about Jesus are the grappling hooks by which the sheer summits of truth can be scaled.

Consequently, those hooks, however sharp, should not be feared. Neither should they be discouraged. For questions are the very hooks by which a person climbs from doubt to faith.

What we want to do in this series of studies is take a time machine to the first century and examine some of those questions. When we do, we will leave behind the reams of research catalogued in seminary libraries, leave behind the shelves of theological books in Christian bookstores, and leave behind two thousand years of church history. We will go back to a time when there were no courses about the life of Christ, no mass market paperbacks about Him, no card catalog entries about Him listed in the Dewey decimal system. We will go back to the rudimentary question: Who is this one they call Jesus?

The Crucial Issue of Christ's Identity

This question brings us to a passage of Scripture from the pen of a man who had been converted from the world of finance to the world of faith. The man is Matthew. And the passage is found in a Gospel he wrote about Jesus after his conversion.

---

2. Elie Wiesel, *Night*, trans. Stella Rodway (New York, N.Y.: Bantam Books, 1960), p. 2.

Now when Jesus came into the district of Caesarea Philippi, He began asking His disciples, saying, "Who do people say that the Son of Man is?" And they said, "Some say John the Baptist; and others, Elijah; but still others, Jeremiah, or one of the prophets." He said to them, "But who do you say that I am?" And Simon Peter answered and said, "Thou art the Christ, the Son of the living God." And Jesus answered and said to him, "Blessed are you, Simon Barjona, because flesh and blood did not reveal this to you, but My Father who is in heaven." (Matt. 16:13–17)

On the heels of this illuminating passage comes the shadow of verse 21.

From that time Jesus Christ began to show His disciples that He must go to Jerusalem, and suffer many things from the elders and chief priests and scribes, and be killed, and be raised up on the third day.

William Barclay shows us how these two passages relate.

The end was coming very near and Jesus needed all the time alone with his disciples that he could gain. He had so much to say to them and so much to teach them, although there were many things which then they could not bear and could not understand.

To that end he withdrew to the districts of Caesarea Philippi. Caesarea Philippi lies about twenty-five miles north-east of the Sea of Galilee. . . .

Confronting Jesus at this time was one clamant and demanding problem. His time was short; his days in the flesh were numbered. The problem was—was there anyone who understood him? Was there anyone who had recognized him for who and what he was? Were there any who, when he was gone from the flesh, would carry on his work, and labour for his kingdom? Obviously that was a crucial problem, for it involved the very survival of the Christian faith. . . .

It is of the most dramatic interest to see *where* Jesus chose to ask this question. There can have been few districts with more religious associations than Caesarea Philippi. . . .

The area was scattered with temples of the ancient Syrian Baal worship. Thomson in *The Land and the Book* enumerates no fewer than fourteen such temples in the near neighbourhood. Here was an area where

3

the breath of ancient religion was in the very atmosphere. Here was a place beneath the shadow of the ancient gods.[3]

Looming tall were monuments and temples of the ancient god Baal. In addition, there was a massive, white marble temple that had been built to the godhead of Caesar. And in the shadows of these intimidating structures stood a penniless King without a kingdom, whose cabinet was composed of fishermen and tax collectors.

The contrast is as dramatic as it is divine. And it is there—of all places—that this brash young carpenter asks men to believe that He is the Son of God.

First Jesus asks what the public consensus is. The opinion poll was divided. A segment believed Him to be John the Baptist. For the birth of that rumor, look at Matthew 14:1–12.

> At that time Herod the tetrarch heard the news about Jesus, and said to his servants, "This is John the Baptist; he has risen from the dead; and that is why miraculous powers are at work in him." For when Herod had John arrested, he bound him, and put him in prison on account of Herodias, the wife of his brother Philip. For John had been saying to him, "It is not lawful for you to have her." And although he wanted to put him to death, he feared the multitude, because they regarded him as a prophet. But when Herod's birthday came, the daughter of Herodias danced before them and pleased Herod. Thereupon he promised with an oath to give her whatever she asked. And having been prompted by her mother, she said, "Give me here on a platter the head of John the Baptist." And although he was grieved, the king commanded it to be given because of his oaths, and because of his dinner guests. And he sent and had John beheaded in the prison. And his head was brought on a platter and given to the girl; and she brought it to her mother. And his disciples came and took away the body and buried it; and they went and reported to Jesus.

Another group believed that Jesus was an incarnation of Elijah, the quintessential prophet who lived nine hundred years earlier. In

3. William Barclay, *The Gospel of Matthew*, rev. ed., The Daily Study Bible Series (Philadelphia, Pa.: Westminster Press, 1975), vol. 2, pp. 133–34. Used by kind permission of The Saint Andrew Press, Edinburgh, Scotland.

the last prophetic word to the nation, the people were told to be on the lookout for Elijah's return.

> "Behold, I am going to send you Elijah the prophet before the coming of the great and terrible day of the Lord. And he will restore the hearts of the fathers to their children, and the hearts of the children to their fathers, lest I come and smite the land with a curse." (Mal. 4:5–6)

Still another group believed Jesus to be Jeremiah, a greatly revered prophet who was also considered a forerunner of the coming Messiah.

Just like opinion polls today, the pendulum of responses swung far and wide. But when Jesus turns the question to His disciples, it's as if all time stands still: "Who do you say that I am?" (Matt. 16:15). A stunned silence ensues, which is promptly filled by Peter, in perhaps the disciple's greatest hour. He blurts out: "Thou art the Christ, the Son of the living God" (v. 15). And the beatitudes Jesus then confers on Peter show that He accepts the confession of faith as a concrete fact.

But Peter was not alone in his convictions. Throughout the centuries others echoed his testimony. Napoleon, Tolstoy, Dickens, C. S. Lewis, just to name a few. Even the philosopher Rousseau made a bold confession when comparing Jesus to Socrates:

> The death of Socrates, peacefully philosophising with his friends, appears the most agreeable that could be wished for; that of Jesus, expiring in the midst of agonising pains, abused, insulted, cursed by a whole nation, is the most horrible that could be feared. Socrates, in receiving the cup of poison, blessed the weeping executioner who administered it; but JESUS, in the midst of excruciating tortures, prayed for his merciless tormentors.
>
> Yes, if the life and death of Socrates were those of a sage, the life and death of JESUS are those of a God.[4]

The Life-Changing Significance of Your Answer

Twentieth-century crowds are as divided regarding the identity of Christ as were first-century crowds. Some say He was a good moral teacher; others say He is Lord. Regarding these differing opinions, C. S. Lewis made these trenchant remarks:

---

4. Jean Jacques Rousseau, as quoted in *Behold the Man*, pp. 193–94.

I am trying here to prevent anyone saying the really foolish thing that people often say about Him: "I'm ready to accept Jesus as a great moral teacher, but I don't accept His claim to be God." That is the one thing we must not say. A man who was merely a man and said the sort of things Jesus said would not be a great moral teacher. He would either be a lunatic—on a level with the man who says he is a poached egg—or else he would be the Devil of Hell. You must make your choice. Either this man was, and is, the Son of God: or else a madman or something worse. You can shut Him up for a fool, you can spit at Him and kill Him as a demon; or you can fall at His feet and call Him Lord and God. But let us not come with any patronising nonsense about His being a great human teacher. He has not left that open to us. He did not intend to.[5]

Of course, the crucial issue is: Who do *you* say that He is?

He is either a liar, a lunatic, or He is who He claimed to be—Lord. Won't you fall before Him as your Lord and Savior?

There is no one else qualified to grant forgiveness. No one else who will never leave or forsake you. No one else who can heal your diseases or dry your tears or calm your anxieties. No one else who can understand your deepest secret or your darkest shame. No one else who can bring back the joy, the love, the tenderness that has been stolen from you by abuse or neglect.

And when you do fall on your knees and bow before Him, expect to be transformed from the inside out.

> Therefore if any man is in Christ, he is a new creature; the old things passed away; behold, new things have come. (2 Cor. 5:17)

◆

Our Father,

We pause at this moment to thank You for the good news of Christ, to thank You for the men and women who have modeled His message and been unashamed to declare their faith. At this moment there are decisions hanging in

5. C. S. Lewis, *Mere Christianity* (New York, N.Y.: Macmillan Publishing Co., 1952), pp. 40–41.

the balance. Some people are so healthy and strong and young, they feel they will be able to put this decision off. Convince them otherwise. Some this very day have never been closer. Bring them to the point of faith.

And, Lord, deepen our relationship with You as a result of the pursuit of these questions and the answers that fit. In the strong name of Jesus Christ, the Son of God, the Messiah, the Lord, the Savior, the King, we pray. Amen.

 ## *Living Insights* STUDY ONE

If you haven't settled that question—"Who do you say that I am?"—in your own mind, won't you do it now? If not, won't you take the time to find the answer to that question? It's the most important one you will ever answer, for your eternal destiny hangs in the balance.

For a vivid reenactment of the life of Christ, get a copy of Fulton Oursler's book *The Greatest Story Ever Told* or the more recent book by Marjorie Holmes titled *The Messiah.*

For a devotional treatment of the life of Christ, there are three books by Max Lucado that are excellent: *No Wonder They Call Him the Savior, God Came Near,* and *Six Hours One Friday.*

For an apologetic treatment of Christ's life, consult *Evidence That Demands a Verdict* by Josh McDowell or *Mere Christianity* by C. S. Lewis.

And for a firsthand, eyewitness account of Christ's life, the Gospel of Mark would be a good book to read.

If you have already settled the issue of Jesus' identity in your mind and made a throne for Him in your heart, won't you take the time now to pray for someone who is still wrestling with that decision?

 ## *Living Insights* STUDY TWO

Second Corinthians 5:17 makes a remarkable promise about a transformed life for all those who have been born again.

Take a step back from that verse and examine the broader context in verses 7–17. In the chart that follows, see how many things you can list that are the vestigial organs of the old creature and how many that are the vital organs of the new creature.

Characteristics of the Old Creature	Characteristics of the New Creature

For additional study, meditate on Romans 8:28–29 and 12:1–2 to find out how that process of transformation takes place in your life.

Chapter 2

WHAT THEN SHALL I DO WITH JESUS?

Matthew 27:11–22

The plot of Harper Lee's novel *To Kill a Mockingbird* revolves around the courtroom trial of an innocent black man unjustly accused of raping a white woman. In spite of his innocence and in spite of the valiant efforts made by his lawyer, Atticus Finch, the fate of the defendant, Tom Robinson, hung in the balance of a parochial and prejudiced jury.

Seen through the eyes of the lawyer's two children, here is the climactic outcome of that trial one hot, summer night in a Maycomb County, Alabama, courtroom.

> A jury never looks at a defendant it has convicted, and when this jury came in, not one of them looked at Tom Robinson. The foreman handed a piece of paper to Mr. Tate who handed it to the clerk who handed it to the judge. . . .
>
> I shut my eyes. Judge Taylor was polling the jury: "Guilty . . . guilty . . . guilty . . . guilty . . ." I peeked at Jem: his hands were white from gripping the balcony rail, and his shoulders jerked as if each "guilty" was a separate stab between them.
>
> Judge Taylor was saying something. His gavel was in his fist, but he wasn't using it. Dimly, I saw Atticus pushing papers from the table into his briefcase. He snapped it shut, went to the court reporter and said something, nodded to Mr. Gilmer, and then went to Tom Robinson and whispered something to him. Atticus put his hand on Tom's shoulder as he whispered. Atticus took his coat off the back of his chair and pulled it over his shoulder. Then he left the courtroom, but not by his usual exit. He must have wanted to go home the short way, because he walked quickly down the middle aisle toward the south exit. I followed the top of his head as he made his way to the door. He did not look up.
>
> Someone was punching me, but I was reluctant to take my eyes from the people below us, and from the image of Atticus's lonely walk down the aisle.

"Miss Jean Louise?"

I looked around. They were standing. All around us and in the balcony on the opposite wall, the Negroes were getting to their feet. Reverend Sykes's voice was as distant as Judge Taylor's:

"Miss Jean Louise, stand up. Your father's passin'."[1]

It is a tragic scene, both in the Pulitzer Prize-winning novel and in the Academy Award-winning movie. For nothing is quite as disturbing as when the gavel of justice falls to flatten the life of an innocent person.

The trials of Jesus were infinitely more tragic. Not only was He innocent of the accusations made against Him, He was totally innocent of *ever* committing a sin. If ever there was a miscarriage of justice, it happened that dark and prejudiced Jerusalem night.

The Background: Overview of the Trials of Christ

In the history of jurisprudence, no trials stand as such blatant affronts to justice as do the trials of Jesus. There were six of them in all, each illegal, without one shred of evidence educed from any of the witnesses. Yet in spite of the groundless accusations, Jesus was sentenced to death. And there was no Atticus Finch to plead His case, for even His closest confidants had deserted Him that fateful night.

Type of Trial: Jewish or Roman?

At the time of Christ, Palestine lumbered along under the yoke of Roman rule. The Jews were allowed to conduct trials under the jurisdiction of a seventy-man ruling body known as the Sanhedrin. But the Sanhedrin did not have the power to execute. Capital punishment required the approval of the Roman government. This explains why the Jews didn't simply march Jesus out of the city and stone Him, as was the Old Testament custom. This also explains why Jesus was brought before the Roman as well as the Jewish authorities.

Formal Accusation: Blasphemy or Treason?

Under Jewish law, the single most devastating charge that could be brought against a prisoner was blasphemy. In Matthew 26:57–66, that was the charge brought against Christ at the trial conducted by the high priest.

---

1. Harper Lee, *To Kill a Mockingbird* (Philadelphia, Pa.: J. B. Lippincott Co., 1960), pp. 193–94.

And those who had seized Jesus led Him away to Caiaphas, the high priest, where the scribes and the elders were gathered together. . . . Now the chief priests and the whole Council kept trying to obtain false testimony against Jesus, in order that they might put Him to death; and they did not find any, even though many false witnesses came forward. But later on two came forward, and said, "This man stated, 'I am able to destroy the temple of God and to rebuild it in three days.'" And the high priest stood up and said to Him, "Do You make no answer? What is it that these men are testifying against You?" But Jesus kept silent. And the high priest said to Him, "I adjure You by the living God, that You tell us whether You are the Christ, the Son of God." Jesus said to him, "You have said it yourself; nevertheless I tell you, hereafter you shall see the Son of Man sitting at the right hand of Power, and coming on the clouds of heaven." Then the high priest tore his robes, saying, "He has blasphemed! What further need do we have of witnesses? Behold, you have now heard the blasphemy; what do you think?" They answered and said, "He is deserving of death!"

The religious authorities wanted to put Jesus to death, so they shuffled Him off to civil authorities.[2]

Now when morning had come, all the chief priests and the elders of the people took counsel against Jesus to put Him to death; and they bound Him, and led Him away, and delivered Him up to Pilate the governor. (Matt. 27:1–2)

For the civil authorities, however, accusations of blasphemy held little weight. Which is why the prosecution changed the charge to treason, the most serious crime that could be committed in the Roman world. Sit in the gallery, as Atticus Finch's children did, and see the dialogue flicker back and forth in that lamplit, Roman courtroom.

They led Jesus therefore from Caiaphas into the Praetorium, and it was early; and they themselves did not enter into the Praetorium in order that they might not be defiled, but might eat the Passover. Pilate therefore went out to them, and said, "What accusation do

---

2. At the conclusion of this lesson a chart documenting the trials of Christ is provided for convenient reference.

you bring against this Man?" They answered and said to him, "If this Man were not an evildoer, we would not have delivered Him up to you." Pilate therefore said to them, "Take Him yourselves, and judge Him according to your law." The Jews said to him, "We are not permitted to put anyone to death," that the word of Jesus might be fulfilled, which He spoke, signifying by what kind of death He was about to die.

Pilate therefore entered again into the Praetorium, and summoned Jesus, and said to Him, "Are You the King of the Jews?" Jesus answered, "Are you saying this on your own initiative, or did others tell you about Me?" Pilate answered, "I am not a Jew, am I? Your own nation and the chief priests delivered You up to me; what have You done?" Jesus answered, "My kingdom is not of this world. If My kingdom were of this world, then My servants would be fighting, that I might not be delivered up to the Jews; but as it is, My kingdom is not of this realm." Pilate therefore said to Him, "So You are a king?" Jesus answered, "You say correctly that I am a king. For this I have been born, and for this I have come into the world, to bear witness to the truth. Everyone who is of the truth hears My voice." Pilate said to Him, "What is truth?" (John 18:28–38a)

Ultimate Verdict: Innocent or Guilty?

The Jewish authorities feared that Pilate would find Jesus innocent —which he did—and then release the brash, young preacher back into the streets where His popularity would increase. Consequently, they were only interested in one verdict—guilty—for that would lead to crucifixion.

Their problem, however, was an absence of evidence, which necessitated pressure in place of proven facts. Let's take a closer look at the case and see how they squeezed the verdict they wanted out of a very reluctant Pilate.

The Case: Analysis of the Interrogation before Pilate

The setting: Early morning, the day before Passover.

The pivotal actor: Pontius Pilate, who served as procurator or governor of Judea from A.D. 26 to 35. He would have been in office six years, which would make him at least in his mid-thirties, since the minimum age for entering the office of procurator was twenty-seven. Pilate was reported to have been sarcastic, unsympathetic, brutal, and decidedly anti-Semitic.

Pressure on Pilate

Much of the pressure on Pilate's life was put there by his own abuse of power, as William Barclay notes in his commentary.

> When Pilate came to Judaea, he found trouble in plenty, and much of it was of his own making. His great handicap was that he was completely out of sympathy with the Jews. More, he was contemptuous of what he would have called their irrational and fanatical prejudices, and what they would have called their principles. The Romans knew the intensity of Jewish religion and the unbreakable character of Jewish belief, and very wisely had always dealt with the Jews with kid gloves. Pilate arrogantly proposed to use the mailed fist.
>
> He began with trouble. The Roman headquarters were in Caesarea. The Roman standards were not flags; they were poles with the Roman eagle, or the image of the reigning emperor, on top. In deference to the Jewish hatred of graven images, every previous governor had removed the eagles and the images from the standards before he marched into Jerusalem on his state visits. Pilate refused to do so. The result was such bitter opposition and such intransigence that Pilate in the end was forced to yield, for it is not possible either to arrest or to slaughter a whole nation.
>
> Later, Pilate decided that Jerusalem needed a better water supply—a wise decision. To that end he constructed a new aqueduct—but he took money from the Temple treasury to pay for it.
>
> Philo, the great Jewish Alexandrian scholar, has a character study of Pilate—and Philo, remember, was not a Christian, but was speaking from the Jewish point of view. The Jews, Philo tells us, had threatened to exercise their right to report Pilate to the Emperor for his misdeeds. This threat "exasperated Pilate to the greatest possible degree, as he feared lest they might go on an embassy to the emperor, and might impeach him with respect to other particulars of his government —his corruption, his acts of insolence, his rapine, his habit of insulting people, his cruelty, his continual murders of people untried and uncondemned, and his

never-ending gratuitous and most grievous inhumanity." Pilate's reputation with the Jews stank; and the fact that they could report him made his position entirely insecure.[3]

Because of this threat, the Jews could simply turn up the thermostat and put the heat on Pilate any time they wanted. Now the heat was on to crucify Jesus.

But Pilate resisted the flame and publicly declared Jesus innocent (John 18:38b). And in order to cool down the simmering crowd, Pilate suggested an alternative.

Issue of Barabbas

It was a custom at that time that, during the Jewish celebration of Passover, a prisoner of the Jews' choice could be released from jail and set free. Pilate offered them a choice between Jesus and Barabbas (Matt. 27:17).

Matthew calls Barabbas "a notorious prisoner" (v. 16); Mark refers to him as an insurrectionist who committed murder (15:7); Luke brands him with insurrection and murder (23:19); and John describes him simply as "a robber" (18:40).

It seems inconceivable that the crowd would choose to free the incorrigible Barabbas over the incorruptible Jesus, but such was the case. Even in spite of Pilate's attempt to soften the crowd by having Jesus scourged, the crowd remained resolute (John 19:1–6).[4]

Message from Pilate's Wife

In Matthew 27:17–19 we find an intriguing interlude involving Pilate's wife Claudia Procula. Listen to how Jim Bishop recreates the episode in his vivid novel *The Day Christ Died.*

> In Pilate's private apartment, high in the southwest tower, Claudia Procula was awakened by the noise of the crowd. The wife of the Governor remained in her big bronze bed, staring through the white netting overhead. The roars from outside sounded surflike. Claudia called her female slave and asked what time it was and what had excited the crowd.

---

3. William Barclay, *The Gospel of Matthew*, rev. ed., The Daily Study Bible Series (Philadelphia, Pa.: Westminster Press, 1975), vol. 2, pp. 358–59. Used by kind permission of The Saint Andrew Press, Edinburgh, Scotland.

4. Matthew tells us that the chief priests and elders persuaded the crowd to choose Barabbas (27:20).

The maid said that is was the third hour of the morning watch (8 A.M.) and that the Procurator was out in the courtyard, listening to a case brought by the Jews against a man named Jesus. Claudia Procula sat up in bed. She remembered that Caiphas had come last night with an urgent matter to present to her husband. And when the clever priest had left, Pilate had explained the case of Jesus to her before she retired.

This woman was a true Roman. She believed in many gods, and she tried hard not to anger any of them. And she had heard from some of her husband's aides about this man Jesus, and of the miracles he had performed among the Jews. Now she was worried because she did not want the fate of this man to rest in Pilate's hands.

It was possible, she knew, that Jesus might be a god come to earth to test the faith and goodness of these fretful people. If that were so, he might be displeased with any Roman who disposed of the case with malice. Claudia Procula, dark hair in disarray, asked for parchment and quill. The servant brought them and the mistress said that she had had a dream about the man Jesus and that her husband must do nothing to hurt him. She wrote: "Have nothing to do with that just man," and sent it out to Pilate.

The message reached him just before he turned away from the crowd at the gate. He read it and frowned and crumpled it in his hand. The eyes of Jesus burned on him. Pontius Pilate, his bearing regal, left the scene and walked off the balcony into his suite of offices.[5]

Question to the People

Do you want to know what haunted Pilate? We see it in the question he blurted out to the people in Matthew 27:22.

> Pilate said to them, "Then what shall I do with Jesus who is called Christ?" They all said, "Let Him be crucified!"

Pilate was tossed back and forth like a dinghy on a frothy sea. His conscience told him there was no evidence to convict Jesus.

---

5. Jim Bishop, *The Day Christ Died* (New York, N.Y.: Harper and Row, Publishers, 1957), p. 247.

The crowd chanted for His blood. His wife warned him not to touch the man.

> And he said, "Why, what evil has He done?" But they kept shouting all the more, saying, "Let Him be crucified!" And when Pilate saw that he was accomplishing nothing, but rather that a riot was starting, he took water and washed his hands in front of the multitude, saying, "I am innocent of this Man's blood; see to that yourselves." And all the people answered and said, "His blood be on us and on our children!" (vv. 23–25)[6]

Thus Pilate tried to wash his hands of the guilt. But there is one thing he couldn't rid himself of, and that is the responsibility. No one had ever stood closer or had more power to change the direction of events regarding Christ's death than Pilate. And he gave in. He buckled under the pressure.

But two thousand years later, the question still remains: *What then shall I do with Jesus Christ?*

The Answer: Response from All Who Ask

If Pilate represents all humanity, there are at least four possible responses to that question.

One: We can be impressed with the person but remain unresponsive.

Two: We can listen to the opinions of others and reject Him.

Three: We can follow the counsel of someone else's superstition or fear.

Four: We can make up our own self-appointed ritual to try to wash our hands of any responsibility in making a decision.

The only answer that will stand up to eternity is the one we give when the roles are reversed and *we* are brought into *God's* courtroom. There we will be impartially judged according to how we have answered—and truly answered—that one, all-important question.

What then will *you* do with Jesus Christ?

---

6. See Deuteronomy 21:6–7, Psalm 26:6a, and 73:13 for the Jewish roots to this symbolic gesture.

---◆---

Our Father,

I know something of what it is to be misunderstood, to be unjustly accused. But I know little of the kind of love that won't struggle against an unfair trial, the kind that would willingly accept the blame for wrongs committed by another.

The times I've been accused of wrongs I haven't done are few and far between. But the times I've been excused of wrongs I have committed are many. Thank You, Jesus, for taking the punishment that was due me. Thank You for facing those cruel fingers of blame so that Your death on the cross could obtain forgiveness for one so undeserving as me.

What will I do with You? I will ask You into my heart, and I will accept with gratitude Your sacrifice. Amen.

 ## *Living Insights*

Imagine yourself being dragged into the courtroom of a totalitarian state that opposes Christianity. The prosecutor has spent the last three months trying to amass evidence that would convict you of being a Christian.

What evidence might be presented to the jury?

_____

_____

_____

_____

What evidence might your defense attorney present to counter the attacks of the prosecutor?

_____

_____

_____

_____

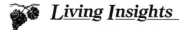

Think back on the time when the jury of your conscience deliberated over the question, What then shall I do with Jesus?

You might have been eight or sixty-eight. But when you came to the verdict that Jesus was who He claimed to be, the case of His identity was forever settled in your heart.

Take a moment now to recall who was most instrumental in helping you recognize Jesus as the Lord and Savior of your life. It may have been a parent, a grandparent, a neighbor, a fellow employee, a Sunday school teacher, a youth leader, a pastor, or a friend. Whoever it was, won't you take a few minutes to thank God for the way He used that person in your life? And if God so prompts you, why not drop that person a note of appreciation?

THE TRIALS OF JESUS CHRIST

Trial	Officiating Authority	Scripture	Accusation	Legality	Type	Result
1	Annas—ex-high priest of the Jews (A.D. 6–15).	John 18:13–23	Trumped-up charges of irreverence to Annas.	ILLEGAL! Held at night. No specific charges. Prejudice. Violence.	Jewish and Religious	Found guilty of irreverence and rushed to Caiaphas.
2	Caiaphas—Annas' son-in-law—and the Sanhedrin (A.D. 18–36).	Matthew 26:57–68 Mark 14:53–65 John 18:24	Claiming to be the Messiah, the Son of God—blasphemy (worthy of death under Jewish law).	ILLEGAL! Held at night. False witnesses. Prejudice. Violence.	Jewish and Religious	Declared guilty of blasphemy and rushed to the Sanhedrin (Jewish supreme court).
3	The Sanhedrin—seventy ruling men of Israel (their word was needed before He could be taken to Roman officials).	Mark 15:1a Luke 22:66–71	Claiming to be the Son of God—blasphemy.	ILLEGAL! Accusation switched. No witnesses. Improper voting.	Jewish and Religious	Declared guilty of blasphemy and rushed to Roman official, Pilate.
4	Pilate, governor of Judea, who was already in "hot water" with Rome (A.D. 26–36).	Matthew 27:11–14 Mark 15:1b–5 Luke 23:1–7 John 18:28–38	Treason (accusation was changed, since treason was worthy of capital punishment in Rome).	ILLEGAL! Christ was kept under arrest, although He was found innocent. No defense attorney. Violence.	Roman and Civil	Found innocent . . . but rushed to Herod Antipas; mob overruled Pilate.
5	Herod Antipas, governor of Galilee (4 B.C.–A.D. 39).	Luke 23:8–12	No accusation was made.	ILLEGAL! No grounds. Mockery in courtroom. No defense attorney. Violence.	Roman and Civil	Mistreated and mocked; returned to Pilate without decision made by Herod.
6	Pilate (second time).	Matthew 27:15–26 Mark 15:6–15 Luke 23:18–25 John 18:39–19:16	Treason, though not proven (Pilate bargained with the mob, putting Christ on a level with Barabbas, a criminal).	ILLEGAL! Without proof of guilt, Pilate allowed an innocent man to be condemned.	Roman and Civil	Found innocent, but Pilate "washed his hands" and allowed Him to be crucified.

Chapter 3

WHY DO YOU SEEK THE LIVING ONE AMONG THE DEAD?

Luke 24:1–9

Have you ever noticed how exact sporting events are? Take basketball, for instance. Carefully preserved lines painted on the polished hardwood floor tell you at any given moment whether you're in bounds or out. Free throw lines tell you just how close you can stand to the basket when shooting foul shots. The half circle that circumscribes the goal tells you if your shot counts for two points or for three. And when the buzzer sounds, everyone knows from the scoreboard who has won and who has lost. If there's a tie, the game goes into overtime until a winner is determined. All the while, officials watch over the game to make sure the rules are impartially enforced and to clarify any close calls.

There is something reassuring about the exactness of an athletic contest. Life, however, is often not so exact.

In today's study we want to take a look at the inexactness of life, and then see how death etches boundary lines in granite to tell us exactly where we will stand in eternity.

Life's Inexact Tensions

When we step out of the sporting arena, life is not so sharply defined. Although society lays down certain rules, often nothing happens when someone steps a little out of bounds or double dribbles or fouls someone else. Seldom are the most valuable players recognized and seldom are the most flagrant violators ever ejected from the game.

From the moment of our birth to the moment of our death, the boundaries of our lives are unsure. Though we may intone marriage vows with resolve, we don't really know the details of our lives—whether we will turn out for better or for worse, for richer or for poorer, or whether we will live in sickness or in health.

Although we may precisely mark our calendars with fine-point pens, we ultimately have little control over what elbows its way into our schedules. We can mark birthdays and anniversaries, but not strokes and cancers. We can set our watches, but we are powerless to stop time's clockwise march.

From the mainspring of a watch to the inner springs of our tightly wound anxieties, we constantly live with tensions. The problem of evil. The problem of the environment. The problem of the economy. The problem of making ends meet.

Nothing seems certain in life—except for death. That is one thing we can count on. No matter what our fate in the here and now, death is the transition that will carry us into our destiny in the hereafter (Heb. 9:27).

The statistics are overwhelming—one out of one dies. And no amount of wealth or power or fame can alter that statistic. The math holds true whether you live on Skid Row or in a Beverly Hills mansion.

Jesus' Controversial Mission

Since we begin life in order to live, it's only natural that we push death out of our conscious minds. Jesus, however, was born to die. The blood He knew He would one day shed formed the outlining paint that would give His mission boundaries and definition. Maybe that is why He was so controversial.

First of all, His birth and childhood were swaddled in controversy. No one had ever been born of a virgin. Who could believe such an impossible thing? But as Luke 1:37 states, "Nothing will be impossible with God."

When the royal birth of God's Son took place, simple strips of cloth were the only robes that adorned the young King (Luke 2:7). These wrappings were similar to the kind used to wrap corpses. So from the moment of His birth, death surrounded the baby Jesus.

His childhood, too, was shrouded in controversy. At only twelve years of age, Jesus confounded the wisest teachers in Israel and left His parents scratching their heads (vv. 41–51).

Unlike us, Jesus knew exactly where He was going. He knew His task was to be about His Father's business (v. 49). He knew precisely the mission for which He had been sent to earth (4:14–21). So articulate was He of His mission that the people stood in awe of Him (v. 22).

His ministry was a maverick one (vv. 42–44, 5:15–16); He was so unlike all the other religious leaders. Instead of flaunting His authority, He demonstrated humility. Instead of seeking popularity, He was content with obscurity. His ministry was a mystery to the established religious order. They didn't know what to do with Him. His healing of the man with a withered hand was just one of the many puzzling experiences they couldn't piece together (6:6–11).

This cycle was repeated time and time again. Jesus continued to do good, and the religious leaders continued to think evil. He continued to heal; they continued to plan His death.

Dorothy Sayers wrote:

> The people responsible for the crucifixion of Jesus never accused him of being a bore—on the contrary: they thought him too dynamic to be safe. It has been left for later generations to muffle up that shattering personality and surround him with a yawning ho-hum atmosphere of tedium. We have efficiently trimmed the claws of the Lion of Judah, certified Him 'meek and mild,' and recommended him as a fitting household pet. . . . To those who knew him, however, he in no way suggested a milk and water person; they objected to him as a dangerous firebrand.[1]

Their objections to this dangerous firebrand reached a fever pitch in Luke 22:1–6, when the religious leaders put a brisk pen to a plot that would write Jesus completely out of the religious scene. While the ink was still wet on the warrant for His arrest, Jesus agonized in prayer in the Garden of Gethsemane at the foot of the Mount of Olives (22:39–44). And while His closest disciples slept, the one whose heart was farthest away betrayed Him (vv. 45–47).

Pummeled with cruel fists and ruthless interrogations, Jesus openly confessed to being the Son of God (vv. 63–71). And then this One who claimed to be deity died (23:44–46, 50–53).

Can you imagine the disillusionment of the disciples?

> His frightened followers huddled in little knots in their rented rooms. Over and over they relived and recounted to each other the drastic events of the preceding week. Each had witnessed the final dreadful drama from a different perspective. So they sat, often in tears, deeply mourning, telling each other their tales of grief. . . .

---

1. Dorothy Sayers, *The Jesus Book,* as quoted by Brennan Manning in *Lion and Lamb* (Old Tappan, N.J.: Fleming H. Revell Co., Chosen Books, 1986), pp. 93–94.

The Master had met an ignominious end.
And for them there was no future.
It was back to the old life.
Back to boats for Peter and his pals. . . .

What none of them knew was the titanic triumphs taking place out beyond the narrow horizons of their little selves. They could not see much beyond their tears and heartache. They were so preoccupied with their own personal problems and grief they could not grasp what was happening at the grave. They were sunk down in sadness. Outside, God was active in great glory.

The divine events of that weekend rival in majestic mystery those stupendous exchanges which took place at Calvary. They are beyond our human capacity to fully comprehend. It was God moving in enormous power, yet without public fanfare or display. It was God achieving His purpose, overwhelming every force set against Him, yet unwitnessed and unheralded except by angelic hosts. . . .

Quickened, enlivened, energized by God the Father, God the Spirit, and God the Son Himself, He simply cast off the constrictions surrounding Him. He was alive in a radiant new dimension of supernatural living, instantaneously.

No man's hands unwrapped those heavy spices around Him.

No man's hands unwound those windings that bound Him.

No man's hands removed the bindings about His face.

No man's hands loosed Him and let Him go.

No man's hands rolled the great rock door away.

No man's hands broke the seal set upon the tomb.

No man's hands struck the guards to the ground outside.

This was only and all the work of God![2]

No night was ever darker than the night that stone was rolled to seal the tomb of the Light of the World. Yet with God nothing shall be impossible. With God there is always the hope of an Easter morning.

2. W. Phillip Keller, *Rabboni . . . Which Is to Say Master* (Old Tappan, N.J.: Fleming H. Revell Co., 1977), pp. 283–84.

Angel's Surprising Question

On that first Easter morning, before the sun brushed the first strokes of dawn across the gray horizon, several women came to Jesus' tomb.

> But on the first day of the week, at early dawn, they came to the tomb, bringing the spices which they had prepared. And they found the stone rolled away from the tomb, but when they entered, they did not find the body of the Lord Jesus. And it happened that while they were perplexed about this, behold, two men suddenly stood near them in dazzling apparel; and as the women were terrified and bowed their faces to the ground, the men said to them, "Why do you seek the living One among the dead? He is not here, but He has risen. Remember how He spoke to you while He was still in Galilee, saying that the Son of Man must be delivered into the hands of sinful men, and be crucified, and the third day rise again." And they remembered His words, and returned from the tomb and reported all these things to the eleven and to all the rest. (24:1-9)

"Why do you seek the living One among the dead?" The question curls around them like a shepherd's staff around the neck of a sheep to gently pull them out of the tomb and send them running to tell the disciples.

Our Possible Options

Only two options exist in the gaping reality of that open tomb. First, we can *reject* it as nonsense, which is what the disciples first did when they heard the news (vv. 10–11). Reality, however, is not formed from the mold of majority opinion. It is shaped by the hands of God. And it is into those hands that we all will one day fall.

> It is appointed for men to die once and after this comes judgment. (Heb. 9:27)

The second option is to *receive* the truth about the death and Resurrection of Christ. Doing so will not spare us from death, but it will deliver us from damnation.

> "Truly, truly, I say to you, he who hears My word, and believes Him who sent Me, has eternal life, and does not come into judgment, but has passed out of death into life." (John 5:24)

If you died tonight, do you know where you would spend eternity? Not think, not hope, but *know*. Do you *know* for sure that heaven will be your eternal home? Look deep into your soul. Has there ever been a time when you said, "Lord Jesus, I come to you as a sinful person, lost in myself, without hope, without the assurance of eternal life, but today I believe that You died and rose from the dead, and today I give You my heart"? Have you told the Savior that?

If not, there is no better time than now. Don't put it off until tomorrow. We never know what tomorrow may bring . . . it may even bring death.

———◆———

Our Father,

> We acknowledge that You are the Lord of life and the God of death. You are the One in control and You are the One in power, and therefore You are the One to whom we speak through Jesus Christ. We pray that You would move upon those who have yet to give their lives to Christ and bring them this day to a knowledge of salvation, to the assurance of a heavenly home.
>
> How grateful we are, our Father, for Your hand upon us. How glorious is Your name for having raised Jesus from the dead. We anticipate the same for everyone who dies. Bring us to the point of decision this very day, Father. For Jesus' sake. Amen.

 Living Insights

Meditate on Psalm 90:1–12. It is a psalm written by Moses in the autumn years when his remaining days clung frailly to the brittle branches of his life.

Now think about your own life. If you found out that this was the last year you had to live, what decisions would you make about your life?

• Regarding your relationship with God:

_____

_____

_____

_____

• Regarding your relationship with your family:

_____

_____

_____

_____

_____

• Regarding your relationship with others, your job, your talents, etc.:

_____

_____

_____

_____

_____

Turn Moses' psalm into a personal prayer, praying that God would teach you, too, to number your days so that you can present to God a heart of wisdom.

Living Insights STUDY TWO

Do you have anything you're presently grieving over? Maybe it's the death of a relationship. Maybe it's the death of a dream. Maybe it's the death of your desires. Whatever it is, it is entirely possible for God to bring new life out of that situation. No matter how dark the tomb or how heavy the stone that seals it.

Regarding His own death, Jesus said: "Truly, truly, I say to you, unless a grain of wheat falls into the earth and dies, it remains by itself alone; but if it dies, it bears much fruit" (John 12:24).

• What is one dead grain you are grieving over?

_____

_____

- What blade of hope can you see sprouting to the surface from that dead grain?

_____

_____

_____

_____

- What fruit can you envision coming from that sprout in the months and years ahead?

_____

_____

_____

_____

- In what ways can that fruit nourish those around you?

_____

_____

_____

_____

Chapter 4
DID NO ONE CONDEMN YOU?
John 8:1–11

Deliverance from condemnation begins with compassion, which is more than pity. Pity is passive. Compassion, on the other hand, is sympathy with its shoes on. It's active and involved.

If you've ever felt condemned and rejected, you know the value of someone else's compassion, of someone who has reached out and helped. Whether you've been physically, emotionally, or spiritually hurt, compassion is the salve of human kindness rubbed into those wounds, the balm that brings about healing and recovery.

A Quality That Makes Life Bearable

Compassion is a quality that makes life bearable. Notice how unbearable were the circumstances over which Jeremiah wept in Lamentations 3.

> Remember my affliction and my wandering, the worm-
> wood and bitterness.
> Surely my soul remembers
> And is bowed down within me. (vv. 19–20)

In spite of his depressing surroundings, Jeremiah remembered something that sparked a flame of hope.

> This I recall to my mind,
> Therefore I have hope.
> The Lord's lovingkindnesses indeed never cease,
> For His compassions never fail.
> They are new every morning;
> Great is Thy faithfulness. (vv. 21–23)

Just as the rising sun radiates the faithfulness of God to warm and brighten His creation, so the Lord's lovingkindnesses and compassions come faithfully to us morning after morning. Our lives, however dark, however cold, always have the hope of His sunshine on the horizon.

The Bible is a record of the kindness and compassion God has shone on His people (see Ps. 136). And the account of the Good

Samaritan in Luke 10 shows how we are to put those qualities to work in our own lives. In that paragraph portrait of compassion, Jesus tells a story to a lawyer that defines who our neighbors are and how we can show them compassion.

> "A certain man was going down from Jerusalem to Jericho; and he fell among robbers, and they stripped him and beat him, and went off leaving him half dead. And by chance a certain priest was going down on that road, and when he saw him, he passed by on the other side. And likewise a Levite also, when he came to the place and saw him, passed by on the other side. But a certain Samaritan, who was on a journey, came upon him; and when he saw him, he felt compassion, and came to him, and bandaged up his wounds, pouring oil and wine on them; and he put him on his own beast, and brought him to an inn, and took care of him. And on the next day he took out two denarii and gave them to the innkeeper and said, 'Take care of him; and whatever more you spend, when I return, I will repay you.' Which of these three do you think proved to be a neighbor to the man who fell into the robbers' hands?" And [the lawyer] said, "The one who showed mercy toward him." And Jesus said to him, "Go and do the same." (vv. 30–37)

Have you ever found yourself kicked, beaten up, left by the side of life's road, and had someone stop and help? If so, you know how important compassion is.

However, the compassion that should flow so freely from our hearts to those in need is often stanched by our perception of that person in need. For example, a shooting victim may evoke less compassion when we find out that he is a gang member; an AIDS victim somehow seems less tragic when we discover her to be a prostitute or an intravenous drug user.

How quick we are to condemn; how slow we are to show compassion.

A Situation That Required Keen Insight

In John 8 we have a perfect example of someone whose checkered past brought sharp condemnation from the crowd.

The Setting

The setting is early morning in Jerusalem, with the dew still on the steps of the temple and purple shadows yawning in the colonnaded courtyard. From the stone corridors echoes the resonant voice of Jesus, teaching the people who have gathered to hear Him speak.

The Trap

Suddenly, without warning, a scheming cohort of stern-faced men push their way into the circle, dragging with them a disheveled woman.

> And the scribes and the Pharisees brought a woman caught in adultery, and having set her in the midst, they said to Him, "Teacher, this woman has been caught in adultery, in the very act. Now in the Law Moses commanded us to stone such women;[1] what then do You say?" And they were saying this, testing Him, in order that they might have grounds for accusing Him. But Jesus stooped down, and with His finger wrote on the ground. (vv. 3–6)

The plan was to entrap Jesus. And what better bait than a helpless woman entangled in a sticky web of Levitical law!

The scribes and Pharisees' religion was a tightly strung corset of rigid rules and regulations. And the freedom Jesus espoused threatened to snap those supposedly sacred strings. Realizing this threat, the religious leaders thought they would test Jesus on one of the more serious tenets of the Law—the law about adultery.

> In the eyes of the Jewish law adultery was a serious crime. The Rabbis said: "Every Jew must die before he will commit idolatry, murder or adultery."[2]

In Greek, the term *caught* in verse 4 means "seized, overcome, overtaken"; it suggests that the men literally pulled the adulterous couple apart. The tense of the verb suggests that those present were the ones who did the catching and that they were still holding the woman in their grasp.

But if that's an accurate picture of what happened, where was her partner? Why didn't they bring the man as well? After all, the Law of Moses addresses both guilty parties. And furthermore, the Talmud and Mishnah, which codify Jewish laws, reiterate the death penalty for both who violate the law. Only the means of death is differentiated: strangulation for the man, stoning for the woman.

1. In verse 5, the religious leaders allude to Deuteronomy 22:22.

2. William Barclay, *The Gospel of John*, rev. ed., The Daily Study Bible Series (Philadelphia, Pa.: Westminster Press, 1975), vol. 2, p. 2.

Three possible options exist regarding her partner:

1. He escaped, which is unlikely. If they seized the woman, they should have been able to seize the man as well.

2. He was deliberately allowed to go free. Since the men's agenda was entrapment and not justice, this certainly would have been possible.

3. The most likely possibility is that the male partner was one of the accusers, put up to the immoral act beforehand to bait the trap.

William Barclay articulates the horns of the dilemma on which the religious leaders sought to impale Christ.

> If he said that the woman ought to be stoned to death, two things followed. First, he would lose the name he had gained for love and for mercy and never again would be called the friend of sinners. Second, he would come into collision with the Roman law, for the Jews had no power to pass or carry out the death sentence on anyone. If he said that the woman should be pardoned, it could immediately be said that he was teaching men to break the law of Moses, and that he was condoning and even encouraging people to commit adultery. That was the trap in which the scribes and Pharisees sought to entrap Jesus.[3]

The Response

Jesus needs to choose His words carefully, so He pauses to gather His thoughts. His reply is one of the most frequently quoted of all the verses in the Bible.

> But when they persisted in asking Him, He straightened up, and said to them, "He who is without sin among you, let him be the first to throw a stone at her." And again He stooped down, and wrote on the ground. And when they heard it, they began to go out one by one, beginning with the older ones, and He was left alone, and the woman, where she had been, in the midst. (vv. 7–9)

Some have suggested that when Jesus stooped down, He was simply doodling in the sand out of embarrassment. But the term John uses is more specific. It is *katagraphō*, which means "to write

3. Barclay, *The Gospel of John*, vol. 2, p. 2.

down." The prefix *kata* can mean "against," as it does in the Greek translation (the Septuagint) of Job 13:26a—"Thou dost write bitter things against me." Possibly Jesus was writing the list of sins the religious leaders had committed. In his sermon "Letters in the Sand," Peter Marshall wrote:

> Looking into their faces, Christ sees into the yesterdays that lie deep in the pools of memory and conscience. He sees into their very hearts, and that moving finger writes on . . .
>
> Idolater . . .
> Liar . . .
> Drunkard . . .
> Murderer . . .
> Adulterer. . . .
>
> There is the thud of stone after stone falling on the pavement.
> Not many of the Pharisees are left.
> One by one, they creep away—like animals—slinking into the shadows . . .
> shuffling off into the crowded streets to lose themselves in the multitudes.[4]

In verses 10–11a John records that magnificent moment of matchless grace, where compassion was as evident as at any time in the Savior's life.

> And straightening up, Jesus said to her, "Woman, where are they? Did no one condemn you?" And she said, "No one, Lord."

The contrast of characters stands out in sharp relief: a sinful woman standing next to a sinless man. The scene illustrates so poignantly that deliverance from condemnation begins with compassion. You see, when legalism and prejudice condemn, violence and hate attack. But when grace and truth confront, love and mercy affirm.

The Counsel

Jesus not only acknowledges this fallen woman's past, He challenges her future:

> And Jesus said, "Neither do I condemn you; go your way. From now on sin no more." (v. 11b)

---

4. Peter Marshall, "Letters in the Sand," as quoted by Catherine Marshall in *A Man Called Peter* (New York, N.Y.: McGraw-Hill Book Co., 1951), p. 325.

The only one without sin, the only one qualified to throw a stone, chose not to. Instead, He gave her words of grace and truth. The story is a beautiful one, but it is unfinished, for every life is unfinished until it stands before God.

The Principles That Continue to Apply

Three principles emerge from this highly sensitive confrontation with the woman caught in adultery. First, confronting wrong calls for understanding and compassion—not cruelty. Second, condemning wrong requires humility and grace—not pride. Third, correcting wrong begins with forgiveness and hope—not rebuke.

The passage about the adulterous woman illustrates a key verse in the prologue to John's Gospel: "For the Law was given through Moses; grace and truth were realized through Jesus Christ" (1:17). Like dipping a bucket into a bottomless well, we can draw "grace upon grace" from the brimming fullness of the Savior's compassion. We can never exhaust the well of grace He has available for us. Never. No matter how serious the sin. And no matter how unworthy we feel to approach Him. He stands waiting to touch our parched lips with His tender mercy.

---◆---

Our Father,

> *Thank You that, while others may have their hands filled with stones of condemnation, You have a heart filled with compassion. Thank You that I can stand before You in the tear-streaked shame of a squandered life and look into Your eyes and there find forgiveness.*
>
> *I am unworthy of so great a love. And in the strength of that unmerited love, may I go my way and sin no more. Amen.*

 Living Insights

Take a few minutes to dig deep into your life to unearth those things for which you feel condemned. Things that have haunted you for years. Things that point a finger at you and accuse you. Things that you're ashamed to talk about with anyone else.

Now instead of raking yourself over the coals, meditate on the compassion of God described in Psalm 103:8–14. And remember, deliverance from condemnation begins with compassion.

The Lord is compassionate and gracious,
Slow to anger and abounding in lovingkindness.
He will not always strive with us;
Nor will He keep His anger forever.
He has not dealt with us according to our sins,
Nor rewarded us according to our iniquities.
For as high as the heavens are above the earth,
So great is His lovingkindness toward those who fear
    Him.
As far as the east is from the west,
So far has He removed our transgressions from us.
Just as a father has compassion on his children,
So the Lord has compassion on those who fear Him.
For He Himself knows our frame;
He is mindful that we are but dust.

 ## Living Insights

Remembering that compassion is sympathy with its shoes on, do a personal study of the Good Samaritan in Luke 10:25–37 and answer the following questions.

- Give a thumbnail character sketch of the two men who failed to aid the man left for dead.

Priest	Levite
_____	_____
_____	_____
_____	_____
_____	_____
_____	_____
_____	_____
_____	_____

- What quality distinguished the Samaritan from the priest and the Levite?

_____

_____

- What rationalizations might the priest and the Levite have made in their minds to keep them from rendering aid?

_____

_____

_____

- List all the things the Samaritan did to show love to this helpless and hurting individual.

_____

_____

_____

- Who is your neighbor? Who around you has fallen among robbers, been stripped and beaten and left for dead? Maybe those responsible weren't actual robbers. Maybe the theft and abuse came from a marriage partner or romantic relationship, a severed friendship or guilt from the past. Whoever or whatever the attackers were, they can leave the person stripped of all self-esteem, wounded in spirit, and drained of all life. Write down the name of a neighbor in need.

_____

- How can you show compassion in a practical way to this person?

_____

_____

_____

_____

_____

Chapter 5

WHO IS THE GREATEST IN THE KINGDOM OF HEAVEN?

Matthew 18:1–6, 10

Conceit, says Webster, is an "excessive appreciation of one's own worth."[1] And as Paul writes, conceit is one of the characteristics of the last days. That word is tucked into the list which appears in the third chapter of 2 Timothy.

> But realize this, that in the last days difficult times will come. For men will be lovers of self, lovers of money, boastful, arrogant, revilers, disobedient to parents, ungrateful, unholy, unloving, irreconcilable, malicious gossips, without self-control, brutal, haters of good, treacherous, reckless, conceited, lovers of pleasure rather than lovers of God. (vv. 1–4)

Notice two of the words in verse 4, "reckless" and "conceited." A reckless person is someone swept on by passion and impulse that circumvent wise thinking. A conceited person is one whose head is swelled with an exaggerated sense of self-importance. Put the two words together and you get "reckless conceit," a quality that's running rampant in our day from athletes to attorneys, from entrepreneurs to entertainers, from politicians to preachers.

Someone once said that pride is the only disease that makes everyone sick except the person who has it. And of all who get sick over it, God gets the most nauseated, as Proverbs 6:16–17 notes:

> There are six things which the Lord hates,
> Yes, seven which are an abomination to Him:
> Haughty eyes, a lying tongue,
> And hands that shed innocent blood. . . .

Topping the list is "haughty eyes," eyes that are filled with arrogance, eyes that look condescendingly on others. As we will see in today's lesson, it is the eyes of a child that capture the Lord's heart—not the eyes of conceit.

---

1. *Webster's Ninth New Collegiate Dictionary*, see "conceit."

Greatness in the World's Eyes

In Paul's first letter to Timothy, the apostle mentions the word *conceit* three times, and each mention reveals something about how the world defines greatness. The first occurrence is in the list of qualifications for an overseer of a church.

> And not a new convert, lest he become conceited and fall into the condemnation incurred by the devil. (3:6)

What does this passage imply? *In the world's eyes we are great if we hold a position of high rank or authority.* The next mention of conceit is in chapter 6.

> If anyone advocates a different doctrine, and does not agree with sound words, those of our Lord Jesus Christ, and with the doctrine conforming to godliness, he is conceited and understands nothing; but he has a morbid interest in controversial questions and disputes about words, out of which arise envy, strife, abusive language, evil suspicions. (vv. 3–4)

From this passage we can see that *in the world's eyes we are great if we have an abundance of knowledge and can outthink others.*

Finally, in verses 9–10 and 17 of the same chapter, we can infer that *in the world's eyes we are great if we are rich and indulge in an extravagant lifestyle.*

> But those who want to get rich fall into temptation and a snare and many foolish and harmful desires which plunge men into ruin and destruction. For the love of money is a root of all sorts of evil, and some by longing for it have wandered away from the faith, and pierced themselves with many a pang. . . . Instruct those who are rich in this present world not to be conceited or to fix their hope on the uncertainty of riches, but on God, who richly supplies us with all things to enjoy.

Note that it is not *having* the money or owning the possessions that is evil, it is *loving* them. The insatiable craving for more is what's wrong.

So in the world's eyes, greatness is having rank, knowledge, or riches. But in God's eyes greatness is measured differently.

The "Greatest" in Heaven's Eyes

To find out how God measures greatness, let's go to Matthew 18.

> At that time the disciples came to Jesus, saying,
> "Who then is greatest in the kingdom of heaven?" (v. 1)

The verse begins with the phrase "At that time"—which begs the question, what time? The parallel account in Mark 9:33–34 gives the context that leads to the question in Matthew 18.

> And they came to Capernaum; and when He was in the house, He began to question them, "What were you discussing on the way?" But they kept silent, for on the way they had discussed with one another which of them was the greatest.

Like children with their hands caught in the cookie jar, the disciples stand silent in the shame of being caught bickering. But they manage to muster enough courage to ask Jesus to settle the debate: "Who then is greatest in the kingdom of heaven?" (Matt. 18:1).

Jesus responds in a disarming way.

> And He called a child to Himself and set him before them, and said, "Truly I say to you, unless you are converted and become like children, you shall not enter the kingdom of heaven. Whoever then humbles himself as this child, he is the greatest in the kingdom of heaven." (vv. 2–4)

How unassuming and unpretentious children are. So playful and naive and innocent. So unimpressed with things like title, IQ, and salary. So unsophisticated and uninhibited.

The word *converted* in verse 3 literally means "turned." It suggests the disciples were headed down the wrong street and needed to make a U-turn. They needed to stop comparing themselves to each other and start comparing themselves to the child who sat on Jesus' lap.

And what are some of those childlike qualities so dear to the Lord? Innocence, the ability to wonder, the capacity to forgive and fully forget. The willingness to learn, the eagerness to do, the contentment to simply be who you are without needing to impress.

Who is greatest in the eyes of heaven? Whoever is as humble as a small child. And part of that humility is seen in a child's total dependence and absolute trust.

That is the way God wants us to be—deferring to Him, leaning on Him, listening to Him, trusting what He says, yielding.

It has been said that the closest thing to heaven is a child. Because that's true, children should be the most treasured of possessions.

That's why we have the positive statement in verse 5 and the negative one in verse 6.

> "And whoever receives one such child in My name receives Me; but whoever causes one of these little ones who believe in Me to stumble, it is better for him that a heavy millstone[2] be hung around his neck, and that he be drowned in the depth of the sea."

There is an interesting connection between verse 5 and Matthew 25:32–40.

> And all the nations will be gathered before Him; and He will separate them from one another, as the shepherd separates the sheep from the goats; and He will put the sheep on His right, and the goats on the left. Then the King will say to those on His right, 'Come, you who are blessed of My Father, inherit the kingdom prepared for you from the foundation of the world. For I was hungry, and you gave Me something to eat; I was thirsty, and you gave Me drink; I was a stranger, and you invited Me in; naked, and you clothed Me; I was sick, and you visited Me; I was in prison, and you came to Me.' Then the righteous will answer Him, saying, 'Lord, when did we see You hungry, and feed You, or thirsty, and give You drink? And when did we see You a stranger, and invite You in, or naked, and clothe You? And when did we see You sick, or in prison, and come to You?' And the King will answer and say to them, 'Truly I say to you, to the extent that you did it to one of these brothers of Mine, even the least of them, you did it to Me.'"

Notice the phrase "the least of them" in verse 40. That's a sign of humility—willing to go to the poorest of the poor and serve them. Our natural desire is to do great things for great people, but there is great reward for doing little things for little people.

As we leaf back a few pages to chapter 18, we find in the Greek of verse 6 that the word changes from *paidion* to *mikros*, from "child" to "little ones."

On these children of faith, whose lives are characterized by innocence, trust, and humility, God places special favor. If their

---

2. Some millstones were hand tools for domestic use, but not this one. This one was a large stone used to crush grain, one that would be pulled by a donkey.

developing legs of faith are tripped up—the Greek verb is *skandalizō*—a harsh penalty will be meted out for the scandalous one responsible.

How seriously does God view the offense of leading an innocent one down an evil path of exploitation, abuse, and destruction? The illustration in verse 6 indicates that the penalty will be harsh. In fact, it would be better for the person to die.

Skipping down to verse 10, we see another severe warning.

> "See that you do not despise one of these little ones,
> for I say to you, that their angels in heaven continually
> behold the face of My Father who is in heaven."

Jesus warns His disciples not to *despise* one of these little ones. The word is used only one other time in Matthew, and that's in 6:24, where Jesus says that a person can't serve two masters, for he will love the one and *despise* the other. Basically, the word means "to think little of." Perhaps *ignore* or *discount* might be acceptable synonyms.

The world's view of children is that they should be seen and not heard, that they only get in the way. God's view is just the opposite. To Him, children are so valuable that each has a specially assigned angel for his or her safekeeping. And not just a private in God's angelic army, but angels who have privileged access to His very throne.

What a statement about the priority God places on children!

To All Who Wish to Be Great

If the question of your own greatness in the kingdom is one you've been wondering about, here are a few suggestions on how to pursue it.

First: *Stay in touch with children.* Spend time with them. Study their ways. Gain a new appreciation for their value in God's eyes.

Second: *Ask God to give you some of their qualities.* Ask Him to give you their innocence, their sense of wide-eyed wonder, their clinging dependency, their humility. Ask Him to deflate your ego, to relax you from the tyranny of the urgent, to release you from the anxiety of competition, to soften you.

Third: *Treat with respect all who emulate the ways of a child.* Be kind to them, even to the least of them. Especially to the least of them. Give them a listening ear. Give them a smile. And most importantly, give them your heart.

———————◆———————

Our Father,

Thank You for being a lover of all children, young and old alike. And in our sophisticated, fast-moving, high-paced, pressurized world, bring us back again to that which truly matters, to the qualities of childlikeness, that we might lose greatness in the eyes of the world but become great in the kingdom of heaven. We pray it in the name of the King. Amen.

 Living Insights

We have learned in this lesson that the world measures greatness by how powerful we are, how smart we are, or how rich we are.

Write down the names of some living people who are great in the world's eyes, based on the above three measurements.

Powerful	Smart	Rich
_____	_____	_____
_____	_____	_____
_____	_____	_____
_____	_____	_____

What do you think will be said about them when they die? Although they may have glowing epitaphs and gilt-edged biographies written about them, what really matters is how *God* views their lives—not how the world views them.

Write the following verses on a 3-by-5-inch card and put it somewhere close so it can be a reminder of what's really important in God's eyes.

Thus says the Lord, "Let not a wise man boast of his wisdom, and let not the mighty man boast of his might, let not a rich man boast of his riches; but let him who boasts boast of this, that he understands and knows Me, that I am the Lord who exercises loving-kindness, justice, and righteousness on earth; for I delight in these things," declares the Lord.
(Jer. 9:23–24)

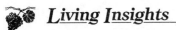 *Living Insights*

List the positive, childlike qualities that have weathered adulthood and remained intact as part of your personality.

_____   _____

_____   _____

_____   _____

_____   _____

What childlike qualities have dropped off en route to your growing up?

_____

_____

Which one do you miss the most?

_____

_____

What could you do to bring that quality back into your life?

_____

_____

_____

_____

On a scale of 1 to 10, 1 being a "bah-humbug" Scrooge and 10 being the "God-bless-us-everyone" Tiny Tim, how would you rate your childlike qualities?

1   2   3   4   5   6   7   8   9   10

What one thing could you do to move that number a notch higher?

_____

_____

_____

_____

To recapture some of the childlike qualities that may have slipped away over the years, why not cuddle up to a children's book and muse over the story and pictures. Try to look at it through the eyes of a child reading it for the first time, instead of through the jaded eyes of an adult. *The Velveteen Rabbit* and *The Polar Express* might be good books to choose.

Chapter 6

WHY ARE YOU SO TIMID?

Mark 4:35–41

W hen Ernest Hemingway was wounded in the First World War," author Ben Patterson tells us, "doctors picked 237 pieces of shrapnel out of his body. As might be expected, he never forgot that experience. But it was not so much the memory of the pain that stayed with him, it was how close he had come to death. He felt that it set him apart from the rest of the human race for the remainder of his life. He recalled the men who shared the experience with him in the convalescent hospital, some of them with faces reconstructed, iridescent and shiny from the work of the plastic surgeons. They too were set apart by their brush with death. They too were suspicious of anyone who had not had the same shattering encounter. Other people seemed trivial and shallow by comparison.

"From this, Hemingway derived a formula for his novels: Put a good man into a situation where he comes face-to-face with death—in the arena fighting a bull, or in combat. Then you will see him in his truest and deepest dimensions. You will find out just how good he really is. The trial will not make or break him, it will reveal him."[1]

Trials do not make or break an individual; they merely reveal the individual. Hemingway's thesis is exemplified in the trial that washed over the disciples on the stormy Sea of Galilee. For it was on that windswept sea that their true colors were revealed, prompting Jesus' question: "Why are you so timid?"

Various Circumstances That Produce Anxiety

Trials and their attendant worries plague all of us. In fact, worry is one thing that sets us apart from the rest of the animal world.

> We are, perhaps, uniquely among the earth's creatures, the worrying animal. We worry away our lives, fearing the future, discontent with the present, unable to take in the idea of dying, unable to sit still.[2]

---

1. Ben Patterson, *Waiting: Finding Hope When God Seems Silent* (Downers Grove, Ill.: InterVarsity Press, 1989), pp. 17–18.

2. Lewis Thomas, as quoted in *Bartlett's Familiar Quotations*, 15th ed., rev. and enl., ed. Emily Morison Beck (Boston, Mass.: Little, Brown and Co., 1980), p. 884.

When worries surround us, we can succumb to anxiety—which can be so severe as to be immobilizing. The categories of worries that steal away our joy and replace it with panic are legion. For instance, *physical conditions.* Shooting pains across our chest. Sudden memory loss. Unexplained headaches. Dizziness. Cancer. The lengthening shadow of death that stretches across our path.

We also worry because of *relational breakdowns.* The threat of a lawsuit. The looming possibility of divorce. The estrangement of a friend or child.

And then there are *personal fears.* The fear of failure, or even of success. The fear of being found out. The fear of assault or of theft. Agoraphobia. Claustrophobia. There are almost two hundred categories of phobias that can crawl over us like ants on a picnic lunch.

And besides these, there are *environmental anxieties.* Earthquakes—the "big one," for Californians. Floods, for Texans. Tornados, for Kansans. Drought, for Iowans. The greenhouse effect. The hole in the ozone layer. Toxic waste. Nuclear energy. The worries are as wide as the earth is round.

As Christians, we are not immune to such worries, regardless of whether they are real or imagined. We, too, can get itchy fingers and press the panic button.

A Classic Example from the First Century

Even the disciples fell apart when their circumstances got out of control, as we will see in Mark 4. The content of the chapter is back-to-back parables—one spiritual lesson after another. But now Jesus takes the disciples out of the lecture hall of theory and into the lab of real life.

> And on that day, when evening had come, He said to them, "Let us go over to the other side." And leaving the multitude, they took Him along with them, just as He was, in the boat; and other boats were with Him. (vv. 35–36)

After a full day of teaching on the western end of the Sea of Galilee, Jesus must have been exhausted. A nice, late-evening sail across the moonlit sea would be a restful and relaxing reprieve.

But the sea they sailed on was subject to sudden storms, as commentator William Hendriksen notes:

> The Sea of Galilee . . . located in the north of the valley of the Jordan, is about thirteen miles in length

45

and seven and one-half miles in width. It lies approximately six hundred eighty feet below the level of the Mediterranean. Its bed is a depression surrounded by hills, especially on the east side with its precipitous cliffs. It is understandable that when the cool currents rush down from Mt. Hermon (9,200 feet) or from elsewhere and through narrow passes between the steep hills [and] collide with the heated air above the lake basin, this downrush is impetuous. The violent winds whip the sea into a fury, causing high waves that splash over bow, side rails, etc., of any vessel that happens to be plying the water surface.[3]

One of those storms struck the disciples' boat that night. So severe was that storm that the parallel account in Matthew uses the word *seismos* to describe it, the same Greek word used for *earthquake.* Mark describes the scene in verse 37.

And there arose a fierce gale of wind, and the waves were breaking over the boat so much that the boat was already filling up.

The word translated "gale" is the Greek word *lailaps.* It refers to a whirlwind or a storm with furious gusts.

But while these seasoned sailors were panicking, Jesus was cuddled up on a cushion in the stern, fast asleep.

And He Himself was in the stern, asleep on the cushion; and they awoke Him and said to Him, "Teacher, do You not care that we are perishing?" (v. 38)

In the midst of the frenzy on the deck and the fury all around, Jesus awoke calm, collected, and controlled. He didn't even raise His voice when He rebuked the rebellious forces of nature.

And being aroused, He rebuked the wind and said to the sea, "Hush, be still." And the wind died down and it became perfectly calm. (v. 39)

A great calm came in the wake of the Master's words. And then those waterlogged fishermen really started to tremble. Jesus turned from the calm of the sea to the anxiety of the sailors and asked a penetrating question.

And He said to them, "Why are you so timid? How is it that you have no faith?" (v. 40)

3. William Hendriksen, *New Testament Commentary: Exposition of the Gospel According to Matthew* (Grand Rapids, Mich.: Baker Book House, 1973), p. 410.

The word *timid* is probably too "timid" a translation from the Greek. The word is actually the term for *coward*, meaning "full of fear and without confidence." The next question supports that translation: "How is it that you have no faith?"

The questions went unanswered. As tiny ripples danced away from the hull like silver ribbons strewn on the sea, the boat rocked from the shaking of the disciples' knees.

> And they became very much afraid and said to one another, "Who then is this, that even the wind and the sea obey Him?" (v. 41)

A greater fear came upon them, because a greater force stood before them.

Some Appropriate Analogies for Today

Such an account is dripping with analogies that tie in beautifully with today's sea of worries. First, *calm evenings frequently lead to stormy nights.* So we shouldn't be lulled into lethargy by the peaceful, idyllic circumstances surrounding us or the rhythmic lapping of a safe, predictable routine.

Second, *sudden surprises can intensify to uncontrollable storms.* It doesn't take long for circumstances you can safely navigate to turn into a typhoon that threatens to destroy you.

Third, *God's silence can be misinterpreted as casual concern.* God cares whether we get shipwrecked and go under. And even if He doesn't always calm the storms around us, He is there to throw us a lifeline.

Fourth, *impossible situations can be calmed only by the Master.* We can take in the sail, man the oars, and bail water; but only Jesus can calm the storm. And the sooner we turn to Him, the sooner we will have peace.

The Next Time Timidity Strikes

The next time anxiety attacks and you feel like panicking, don't reach for the medicine cabinet—rely on the following three-way prescription instead.

Refuse to allow yourself to be controlled by the situation.

Remind yourself of what you believe and what you know.

Replace fear of the seen with faith in the unseen.

Our Father,

In this hour of quietness, we acknowledge Jesus as Lord and we place ourselves without reservation at His disposal. Find within us hearts ready to acknowledge You as sovereign over our lives. Help us to be people of humility and trust, whose faith, when tested, stands strong. We pray in the powerful name of Christ who stilled the storm. Amen.

Living Insights

What storm is presently blowing over the bow of your life?

_____

_____

How would you describe that storm?

☐ a tempest in a teapot

☐ a stiff headwind

☐ a forceful but not fatal gale

☐ ten-foot waves, and I'm bailing as fast as I can

☐ Hurricane Hugo, and I'm about to jump ship

What is the worst thing you fear could happen to you during that storm?

_____

_____

_____

What strategy makes the most sense to get you through the storm?

☐ row harder

☐ bail faster

☐ jump overboard

☐ call out to Jesus

Jesus is the master of the wind and the waves, and as sure as He calmed the storm on the sea, He can calm the storm in your life. Pray through Psalm 46 and see if that doesn't help still the troubled waters in your life.

God is our refuge and strength,
A very present help in trouble.
Therefore we will not fear, though the earth should
    change,
And though the mountains slip into the heart of the
    sea;
Though its waters roar and foam,
Though the mountains quake at its swelling pride.
There is a river whose streams make glad the city of
    God,
The holy dwelling places of the Most High.
God is in the midst of her, she will not be moved;
God will help her when morning dawns.
The nations made an uproar, the kingdoms tottered;
He raised His voice, the earth melted.
The Lord of hosts is with us;
The God of Jacob is our stronghold.
Come, behold the works of the Lord,
Who has wrought desolations in the earth.
He makes wars to cease to the end of the earth;
He breaks the bow and cuts the spear in two;
He burns the chariots with fire.
"Cease striving and know that I am God;
I will be exalted among the nations, I will be exalted
    in the earth."
The Lord of hosts is with us;
The God of Jacob is our stronghold.

 Living Insights   STUDY TWO

Sometimes seeing others survive tempestuous trials gives us the strength to weather our own. This is the story of the storm that ruthlessly washed over Horatio G. Spafford.

Some months prior to the Chicago Fire of 1871, Spafford had invested heavily in real estate on the shore of Lake Michigan, and his holdings were wiped out by this disaster. Just before this he had experienced the death of his son. Desiring a rest for his wife and four daughters as well as wishing to join and assist Moody and Sankey in one of their [evangelistic] campaigns in Great Britain, Spafford planned a European trip for his family in 1873. In November of that year, due to unexpected last minute business developments, he had to remain in Chicago; but he sent his wife and four daughters on ahead as scheduled on the S. S. *Ville du Havre*. He expected to follow in a few days. On November 22 the ship was struck by the *Lochearn*, an English vessel, and sank in twelve minutes. Several days later the survivors were finally landed at Cardiff, Wales, and Mrs. Spafford cabled her husband, "Saved alone." Shortly afterward Spafford left by ship to join his bereaved wife. It is speculated that on the sea near the area where it was thought his four daughters had drowned, Spafford penned this text with words so significantly describing his own personal grief.[4]

> When peace, like a river, attendeth my
> way,
> When sorrows like sea billows roll—
> Whatever my lot, Thou hast taught me
> to say,
> It is well, it is well with my soul.[5]

The next time sea billows roll over your life, think of Spafford's storm and the trust he had in God to calm his troubled soul. Maybe it will help your heart to be filled with a song rather than with worry.

4. Kenneth W. Osbeck, *101 Hymn Stories* (Grand Rapids, Mich.: Kregel Publications, 1982), p. 127.

5. Horatio G. Spafford, "It Is Well with My Soul," as quoted in *101 Hymn Stories,* p. 126.

Chapter 7

WHAT IS YOUR NAME?

Mark 5:1–20

In his classic work *The Screwtape Letters,* C. S. Lewis fictionalized an ongoing correspondence between a senior devil, Screwtape, and his ambitious demon nephew, Wormwood. In this excerpt from one of the letters, Screwtape counsels his nephew on an important point of strategy regarding the Christian patient under Wormwood's jurisdiction.

> My Dear Wormwood,
>   I wonder you should ask me whether it is essential to keep the patient in ignorance of your own existence. That question, at least for the present phase of the struggle, has been answered for us by the High Command. Our policy, for the moment, is to conceal ourselves. . . . I do not think you will have much difficulty in keeping the patient in the dark. The fact that "devils" are predominantly *comic* figures in the modern imagination will help you. If any faint suspicion of your existence begins to arise in his mind, suggest to him a picture of something in red tights, and persuade him that since he cannot believe in that (it is an old textbook method of confusing them) he therefore cannot believe in you.[1]

In today's lesson we want to look beyond the Halloween masks and cute little costumes to see the devil for who he really is. Understanding his identity may send chills down your spine, but it may also give you the backbone to stand up to him and his diabolical schemes.

Getting the Enemy in Proper Focus

No enemy was ever resisted effectively until brought into focus. A favorite strategy of any enemy is to promote misinformation, which blurs the focus and obscures the truth. Mythology, literature, and traditions have all distorted the reality of our enemy, Satan. In

---

1. C. S. Lewis, *The Screwtape Letters* (New York, N.Y.: Macmillan Publishing Co., 1961), pp. 32–33.

fact, three common mistakes people make concerning the devil are (1) they don't believe he exists, (2) they don't take him seriously, or (3) they surrender to his control. To get him in focus, let's first take a look at what he isn't, and then examine what he is.

What He Is Not

The devil is *not* a nobody. He exists and is engaged in an aggressive strategy of persuasion. He also is not a comic character. He isn't an imp with horns and a pitchfork, dressed in red tights. Furthermore, he isn't all-powerful. His power is formidable but not unlimited. His influence is pervasive but not omnipresent.

What He Is

He truly is alive and well on planet earth. He is relentlessly at work, invisible, deceptive, and brilliant. And serving under him is a power structure of demons ready to do his bidding. He is anything but amusing. His work is wicked. His strategies are sinister. But although he is the god of this world, he is limited in his authority. And as Christians, we have no reason to feel afraid, victimized, or intimidated (1 John 4:4).

Confronting the Enemy through Christ's Power

Turning to Mark 5, we encounter one of the most vivid and gripping portraits of evil in the entire Bible. The first person we meet in the opening verses of this chapter is the devil's prisoner.

The Victim

> And they came to the other side of the sea, into the country of the Gerasenes. And when He had come out of the boat, immediately a man from the tombs with an unclean spirit met Him, and he had his dwelling among the tombs. And no one was able to bind him anymore, even with a chain; because he had often been bound with shackles and chains, and the chains had been torn apart by him, and the shackles broken in pieces, and no one was strong enough to subdue him. And constantly night and day, among the tombs and in the mountains, he was crying out and gashing himself with stones. (vv. 1–5)

This graphic picture is hard to look at. Barely a vestige of humanity remains. This man roams about the tombs like an animal, naked and wild (Luke 8:27).

The man was *demonized*,[2] hopelessly and helplessly under the domination of demonic powers. His body was so controlled by satanic influences that it was merely a base of operation for the demons. Even his vocal chords were under their control.

The Deliverance

> And seeing Jesus from a distance, he ran up and bowed down before Him; and crying out with a loud voice, he said, "What do I have to do with You, Jesus, Son of the Most High God? I implore You by God, do not torment me!" For He had been saying to him, "Come out of the man, you unclean spirit!" And He was asking him, "What is your name?" And he said to Him, "My name is Legion; for we are many." And he began to entreat Him earnestly not to send them out of the country. Now there was a big herd of swine feeding there on the mountain. And the demons entreated Him, saying, "Send us into the swine so that we may enter them." And He gave them permission. And coming out, the unclean spirits entered the swine; and the herd rushed down the steep bank into the sea, about two thousand of them; and they were drowned in the sea. (Mark 5:6–13)

The verb tense in verse 8—"had been saying"—indicates that Jesus had taken the initiative and had repeated the command. Apparently the entrenchment of evil was so tenacious that its uprooting took more than one command, even from Jesus.[3]

So He changed His approach and asked a simple, direct question: "What is your name?" The answer sounds puzzling to us: "My name is Legion." A Roman legion equaled 6,826 men. How many are in this legion, we don't know, but it's safe to say at least two thousand, judging by the number of pigs that served as hosts to these wicked parasites (v. 13).

---

2. *Demonized* is a preferable term to *demon-possessed*. "Confusion has been introduced by translating this participle as 'demon possessed.' The word *possession* implies ownership. Actually, demons own nothing. The New Testament regards them as squatters or invaders of territory that does not belong to them. In reality God owns *them*, for He is their Creator and their Judge. Such a faulty translation, then, misleads people regarding the state of the demonized person and causes undue consternation and terror in the hearts of the afflicted and those concerned for him." C. Fred Dickason, *Demon Possession and the Christian* (Chicago, Ill.: Moody Press, 1987), p. 38.

3. See Mark 9:14–29 for a demon so entrenched that the disciples couldn't cast it out.

It's interesting to note how much these demons knew. They knew that Jesus was the Son of the Most High God; they knew His power was greater than theirs; they knew their final destiny ("the abyss," Luke 8:31), as well as the time they would be sentenced there (see Matt. 8:29); and they knew they'd rather indwell an animal than exist without a body (Mark 5:10–12).

The Results

> And their herdsmen ran away and reported it in the city and out in the country. And the people came to see what it was that had happened. And they came to Jesus and observed the man who had been demon-possessed sitting down, clothed and in his right mind, the very man who had had the "legion"; and they became frightened. And those who had seen it described to them how it had happened to the demon-possessed man, and all about the swine. And they began to entreat Him to depart from their region. And as He was getting into the boat, the man who had been demon-possessed was entreating Him that he might accompany Him. And He did not let him, but He said to him, "Go home to your people and report to them what great things the Lord has done for you, and how He had mercy on you." And he went away and began to proclaim in Decapolis what great things Jesus had done for him; and everyone marveled. (vv. 14–20)

The first result was that the man was instantly changed. He was no longer out of control, but sitting; he was no longer naked, but clothed; he was no longer crazy, but in his right mind (v. 15a). Second, the people were at first fearful, then resentful (vv. 15c, 17).[4] The third result was that the man became a witness for Christ (vv. 18–20).

What a revolutionary change—from an evil man to an evangelist!

Overcoming the Enemy with Consistent Effectiveness

Ephesians 6:10–18 gives us an excellent strategy for standing firm against the schemes of Satan.

> Finally, be strong in the Lord, and in the strength of His might. Put on the full armor of God, that you may be able to stand firm against the schemes of the

4. Similar resentment occurred in Acts 16:16–19, where a young fortune-telling woman was delivered from demons, which resulted in a loss of profit for her masters.

devil. For our struggle is not against flesh and blood, but against the rulers, against the powers, against the world forces of this darkness, against the spiritual forces of wickedness in the heavenly places. Therefore, take up the full armor of God, that you may be able to resist in the evil day, and having done everything, to stand firm. Stand firm therefore, having girded your loins with truth, and having put on the breastplate of righteousness, and having shod your feet with the preparation of the gospel of peace; in addition to all, taking up the shield of faith with which you will be able to extinguish all the flaming missiles of the evil one. And take the helmet of salvation, and the sword of the Spirit, which is the word of God. With all prayer and petition pray at all times in the Spirit, and with this in view, be on the alert with all perseverance and petition for all the saints.

First, *we need to put on the full armor of God.* Second, *we need to resist the enemy through the power of God.* Third, *we need to walk in faith by the Spirit of God.*

We close with a final word from Uncle Screwtape, which should encourage us to remember that we are fighting a winnable war.

Do not be deceived, Wormwood. Our cause is never more in danger than when a human, no longer desiring, but still intending, to do our Enemy's will, looks round upon a universe from which every trace of Him seems to have vanished, and asks why he has been forsaken, and still obeys.[5]

————◆————

Holy Father,

When You ask me my name, I want to answer, Christian. I want to declare here and now that I submit to Your authority, and not to the service of the prince of darkness. Please, Lord, dethrone the enemy in my life. Cleanse me from my sin. Help me daily to put on Your armor, so that I might resist Satan's schemes and walk by faith in You.

I acknowledge, Father, that You are mighty in word and deed, and that You are the victor over the enemy of

5. Lewis, *The Screwtape Letters*, p. 39.

*my soul. I thank You for my redemption and for the power
I have in Your Holy Spirit. Amen.*

 Living Insights

In C. S. Lewis' *The Screwtape Letters,* Uncle Screwtape offers his nephew a little advice on the goal and strategy of temptation.

> You will say that these are very small sins; and doubtless, like all young tempters, you are anxious to be able to report spectacular wickedness. But do re-member, the only thing that matters is the extent to which you separate the man from the Enemy. It does not matter how small the sins are, provided that their cumulative effect is to edge the man away from the Light and out into the Nothing. Murder is no better than cards if cards can do the trick. Indeed, the safest road to Hell is the gradual one—the gentle slope, soft underfoot, without sudden turnings, without mile-stones, without signposts.
>
> Your affectionate uncle
> Screwtape[6]

Name some of the small sins or distractions that have edged you away from the Light.

_____

_____

_____

_____

Put a check by one of the most lethal of those small sins and make a conscious effort to eliminate it from your life this week. It may not even be something that is inherently sinful. It may be something so small as late-night TV or the morning newspaper. Whatever it is, if it distracts you from the Savior, it will lessen the quality of your life both in this world and the next.

6. Lewis, *The Screwtape Letters,* p. 56.

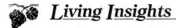 *Living Insights*

Get a copy of *The Screwtape Letters* and read it this week. If your local bookstore doesn't have it, check with the public library. Lewis' book will open your eyes to the invisible war that is being waged day after day for your heart.

As you read, try to discern how Satan has designed a strategy specifically for you.

Also, read through the chart at the end of this chapter to further acquaint yourself with the biblical examples of demonic involvement.

DEMON CONTACT IN

This chart is limited to actual accounts of demonic contact

Scripture	Victim	Tormentor	Victim's Experience
Matthew 4:24	Unnamed sick people.	Demon.	Demonized.
Matthew 8:16 Mark 1:32–34 Luke 4:40–41	Many who were demonized and sick.	Demon, spirit.	Demonized.
Matthew 18:28–34 Mark 5:1–20 Luke 8:26–39	A certain man.	Demons—unclean spirits named Legion.	Demonized. Lived near tombs. Naked. Superhuman strength. No rest. Seizures. Suicidal attacks. No restraint.
Matthew 9:32–33	"A dumb man."	Demon.	Demonized. Unable to speak.
Matthew 12:22	A man.	Demon.	Demonized. Blind and dumb.
Matthew 15:22–28 Mark 7:24–30	A Gentile woman's daughter.	Demon, unclean spirit.	Cruelly demonized.
Matthew 17:14–20 Mark 9:14–29 Luke 9:37–43	A man's only son.	Spirit, demon, unclean spirit.	Mute. Very ill. Suicidal. Seizures. Convulsions. Screaming. Had this "from childhood."
Mark 1:23–27 Luke 4:31–35	"A man."	Unclean spirit, unclean demon.	Cried out. Demon knew Jesus as "Jesus of Nazareth . . . the Holy One of God."
Mark 3:10–11	Many who had afflictions.	Unclean spirits.	Unclean spirits beheld Jesus and cried out: "You are the Son of God!"
Mark 16:9 Luke 8:2	"Some women," Mary Magdalene.	Demons, evil spirits.	Mary had seven demons.

NOTE: There are two descriptive titles used to denote the presence of Satan's workers. One is *demon*, which is from a Greek word meaning "knowing" or "intelligence." A demon is a "knowing one." Intelligence is the most prominent characteristic among demons. Their superior knowledge is used to frustrate God's work and also serves to attract the interest of humans. The other title is *spirit*, which tells us that demons do not possess a material body of flesh and bones (see Luke 24:39). They are,

THE NEW TESTAMENT

with humans for the purpose of affliction and torment.

Method Used to Expel Demons	Demons' Response	Final Result
Jesus "healed them."		Healing.
Laid hands on victims. Cast out with a word. Rebuked the demons.	Cried out, "You are the Son of God!"	Healing.
Talked with demons. Asked for name—"Legion." "Come out . . . , you unclean spirit!" "Begone!" Granted demons' request.	Knew Jesus was the Son of God. Requested to enter swine. Came out and entered swine.	Complete relief. Clothed, resting. In right mind. (Swine drowned.)
Demon was "cast out."		Man was able to speak.
"He healed him."		Man was able to speak and see.
"Healed at once." (Daughter was not present.)	Departed.	Child was lying on her bed. The demon was gone.
Rebuked unclean spirit. Healed the boy. "I command you, come out . . . do not enter him again!"	Cried out. Threw victim into terrible convulsions, departed.	The boy was cured at once. Became quiet "like a corpse."
Jesus rebuked him: "Be quiet and come out of him!"	Threw victim down, caused him convulsions, but did no harm to victim. Came out.	Complete relief.
He healed many.	Fell down before Him.	Healing.
Cast out; healed of evil spirits.		Healing.

Chart continued on next page

however, able to enter in and assume control of a human body, speaking and acting through it from time to time. This title also tells us that demons are not normally subject to human visibility or other sensory perceptions. Their invisibility makes their presence insidious and hard to detect. The word *evil* denotes labor, pain, and sorrow—that which is destructive and injurious. The term *unclean* denotes impurity, filthiness, and defilement.

Scripture	Victim	Tormentor	Victim's Experience
Luke 6:17–18	Great throng of people.	Unclean spirits.	Troubled.
Luke 7:21	Many people.	Evil spirits.	
Luke 11:14–26	A man.	Demon, unclean spirit.	Mute—unable to speak.
Luke 13:10–17	A woman— "a daughter of Abraham."	Spirit.	"A sickness caused by a spirit . . . bent double, and could not straighten up at all." Lasted eighteen years.
Acts 5:16	People who were afflicted.	Unclean spirits.	Affliction.
Acts 8:7	Many people.	Unclean spirits.	
Acts 13:6–11 *	A certain magician, Bar-Jesus.		Sought to turn another away from the faith.
Acts 16:16–18	"A certain slave-girl."	"A spirit of divination."	Persistent crying out, hindering the gospel.
Acts 19:11–16	Unnamed individuals, a man.	Evil spirit.	Violent, superhuman strength.

*This person is not specifically described as having a demon, but the pattern seems very similar to that of demonic contact.

Method Used to Expel Demons	Demons' Response	Final Result
"Being cured."		Cured.
"Cured."		Cured.
"Casting out."		"The dumb man spoke."
Laid hands on her. "Woman, you are freed from your sickness."		Immediately she was made erect, glorified God, and was healed.
		Healing.
	"They were coming out of them shouting with a loud voice."	Healing.
Severe, sudden rebuke by Paul. Blindness pronounced.		The other person believed in Christ.
Paul rebuked it: "I command you in the name of Jesus Christ to come out of her!"	Instantly came out.	Girl was released, and was no longer able to tell fortunes.
Unqualified men, the "seven sons of one Sceva, a Jewish high priest," tried to cast out the evil spirit.	Evil spirit recognized Jesus and Paul, but not these men. The demonized man leaped on and overpowered all seven men.	The "deliverers" fled, naked and wounded.

Chapter 8

WHAT DO YOU SEE?

Mark 8:22–26

Helen Keller was unable to see, hear, or speak. Hers was a lonely world of darkness and silence. That is, until Annie Sullivan came into her life when she was six. Listen to how poignantly Miss Keller told of the first meeting with her teacher.

> Have you ever been at sea in a dense fog, when it seemed as if a tangible white darkness shut you in, and the great ship, tense and anxious, groped her way toward the shore with plummet and sounding-line, and you waited with beating heart for something to happen? I was like that ship before my education began, only I was without compass or sounding-line, and had no way of knowing how near the harbour was. "Light! give me light!" was the wordless cry of my soul, and the light of love shone on me in that very hour.
>
> I felt approaching footsteps. I stretched out my hand as I supposed to my mother. Some one took it, and I was caught up and held close in the arms of her who had come to reveal all things to me, and, more than all things else, to love me.[1]

In a similarly transforming way, Jesus came into the life of a blind man in the quiet village of Bethsaida. That man's experience is a perfect picture of our own spiritual condition. While we were lost, we were spiritually blind (2 Cor. 4:4). But one day, when Jesus crossed our path, our blindness was taken away. And though at first we didn't see everything fully and clearly, little by little our spiritual vision became more focused.

A Proof of Jesus as Messiah

The healing of blindness was one of the ways people of Jesus' day were to know that the true Messiah was among them. When questioned about His identity, Jesus responded by matching His resumé with the job description of the Messiah. The fit was perfect.

---

1. Helen Keller, as quoted in *Turning Point*, ed. Philip Dunaway and George de Kay (New York, N.Y.: Random House, 1958), pp. 105–6.

And when the men had come to Him, they said, "John the Baptist has sent us to You, saying, 'Are You the Expected One, or do we look for someone else?'" At that very time He cured many people of diseases and afflictions and evil spirits; and He granted sight to many who were blind. And He answered and said to them, "Go and report to John what you have seen and heard: the blind receive sight, the lame walk, the lepers are cleansed, and the deaf hear, the dead are raised up, the poor have the gospel preached to them. And blessed is he who keeps from stumbling over Me." (Luke 7:20–23)

A Miracle That Took Time: Seeing Everything Clearly

In the majority of cases recorded in Scripture, Jesus restored sight to the blind instantaneously. But in the passage we will study today, the restoration of vision took time.

The Surrounding Context

Earlier in Mark 8, thousands were fed by Jesus on just seven loaves of bread and a few fish (vv. 1–10). This prompted an argument from the more skeptical Pharisees who wanted to see further proof of His identity in the form of some "sign from heaven" (vv. 11–13). Refusing their request, Jesus leaves His critics and turns His attention to His companions.

And they had forgotten to take bread; and did not have more than one loaf in the boat with them. And He was giving orders to them, saying, "Watch out! Beware of the leaven of the Pharisees and the leaven of Herod." And they began to discuss with one another the fact that they had no bread. And Jesus, aware of this, said to them, "Why do you discuss the fact that you have no bread? Do you not yet see or understand? Do you have a hardened heart? Having eyes, do you not see? And having ears, do you not hear? And do you not remember, when I broke the five loaves for the five thousand, how many baskets full of broken pieces you picked up?" They said to Him, "Twelve." "And when I broke the seven for the four thousand, how many large baskets full of broken pieces did you pick up?" And they said to Him, "Seven." And He was saying to them, "Do you not yet understand?" (vv. 14–21)

The disciples' eyes were dim to the glowing Presence of deity that stood among them. They grasped only the visible, only the plain and obvious realities. They walked by sight, not by faith (see 2 Cor. 5:7). They conducted their lives in the dark, groping around like people who were blind.

The Blind Man

The spiritual blindness of the disciples is juxtaposed to the physical blindness of the man from Bethsaida in Mark 8:22–26.

> And they came to Bethsaida. And they brought a blind man to Him, and entreated Him to touch him. And taking the blind man by the hand, He brought him out of the village; and after spitting on his eyes, and laying His hands upon him . . . (vv. 22–23a)

We're not told how long the blind man had lived in darkness; only that he was brought to Jesus by the disciples, who pleaded with Him to touch the man. A similar incident had occurred earlier, in Mark 7:31–37. It's as though the disciples were anxious for Jesus to verify His identity—"Show them, Lord! Let the people realize who You really are!"

With gentleness and sensitivity our Lord slips away from the curiosity of the crowd and finds a quiet place to be alone with this man. Never once has he seen the face of Jesus or the beauty of His creation. But there is one thing he knows better than sight—he knows *touch*. And it is the Savior's compassionate touch that transforms him.

The Crucial Question

After Jesus touches the man, He poses a crucial question: "Do you see anything?" (8:23b). It's a process question, designed to make the man realize that God is doing something miraculous within him.

There are times in all of our lives when we sense God's touch, when we become sensitive to His hand and become filled with a mixture of thrill, fear, and gratitude. Such is the first rush of feelings that flows through the man as he answers Jesus' question.

> And he looked up and said, "I see men, for I am seeing them like trees, walking about." (v. 24)

The Ultimate Change

At first, the man's sight is indistinct and uncertain. What his blurred vision needs is a corrective adjustment.

Then again [Jesus] laid His hands upon his eyes; and
he looked intently and was restored, and began to see
everything clearly. And He sent him to his home,
saying, "Do not even enter the village." (vv. 25–26)

What did it take for this man's vision to become sharp and clear?
It took a second touch from the Savior's hand.

A Gradual Process: Ever-expanding Vision

In this day of instant gratification and a desire for split-second
miracles, anything that smacks of a gradual or long-term process
doesn't interest us. But sometimes God's best work takes time. Often,
the more deeply things are imbedded within us, the more they need
a second touch from God. That is when vision gets expanded. That
is when we get focus and perspective.

The blind man needed a second touch to restore his physical sight.
In what way do you need a second healing touch? Have you been
wounded emotionally? Maybe you've been abused or neglected or mis-
treated; perhaps devalued, overlooked, despised, or misunderstood.

You may need a second touch on that wound. Without it, you will
grow embittered in the years to come. The hurt will evolve to anger,
the anger to resentment, and the resentment to bitterness. Like a
festering sore, the pain will only burrow deeper; it won't go away.

When Jesus touches this festered area of your life, all the painful
feelings will ooze to the surface, where you will be able to deal with
them. That's when the healing will start. And that's when you will
be able to forgive.

Another area that might need a second touch is the area of
priorities. Are your priorities straight? Do you really have first things
first? Do the things that matter most get the most attention? If not,
why not put that list in the Lord's hand; let Him rearrange it.

What do your priorities reflect about you? Is your world narrow
and selfish? Do you live for today or for eternity? Do you live for
some god of yesterday or some god of tomorrow, rather than for Him
who is the same yesterday, today, and tomorrow?

Or do you worship the gods of money and materialism? Do they
captivate your attention? Do they own your heart? Do they drive
you? Do they dictate how you invest your life?

These are painfully probing questions. But they will help give
clarity to spiritual vision that is blurred. And with a second touch
of the Savior's hand, these blind spots can be healed.

Our Father,

Thank You for these moments of quietness where we have been encouraged to see what we have refused to look at for so long. As we meditate on this story of Jesus' gentle touch, may we do more than read about it and talk about it. May we act upon what we know of Your healing power. Help us with the blind spots in our lives, Lord. Help us to see. Touch us. Heal us. In Jesus' name we pray. Amen.

 ## *Living Insights*

Let's stop to answer the questions raised at the end of this study so that we can expand our vision.

1. Have you been wounded emotionally in some way? If so, describe the wound and the accompanying pain.

_____

_____

_____

Now take the pain to Jesus (see Matt. 9:28–29).

2. Are your priorities straight? If not, what is it that will have to be moved out of first place?

_____

According to Luke 10:38–42, what should be number one on your list of priorities?

_____

3. Do you tend to be preoccupied with *your* money and *your* things?

☐ Yes   ☐ No

If so, it may be time to remind yourself that God owns it all (see Ps. 24:1, Job 1:21). Look up the following passages and see if they can help sharpen your focus in this area of your life.

    Matthew 6:19–34   Philippians 2:3–4

    Luke 12:13–21   1 Timothy 6:7–11

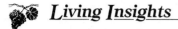

As you read the following excerpt, which comes from Helen Keller's reminiscences of the first words Annie Sullivan taught her, think back on your first stirring of faith when you received your spiritual sight.

> We walked down the path to the well-house, attracted by the fragrance of the honeysuckle with which it was covered. Some one was drawing water and my teacher placed my hand under the spout. As the cool stream gushed over one hand she spelled into the other the word *water,* first slowly, then rapidly. I stood still, my whole attention fixed upon the motions of her fingers. Suddenly I felt a misty consciousness as of something forgotten—a thrill of returning thought; and somehow the mystery of language was revealed to me. I knew then that "w-a-t-e-r" meant the wonderful cool something that was flowing over my hand. That living word awakened my soul, gave it light, hope, joy, set it free! There were barriers still, it is true, but barriers that could in time be swept away. . . .
>
> I learned a great many new words that day. I do not remember what they all were; but I do know that *mother, father, sister, teacher* were among them—words that were to make the world blossom for me, "like Aaron's rod, with flowers." It would have been difficult to find a happier child than I was as I lay in my crib at the close of that eventful day and lived over the joys it had brought me, and for the first time longed for a new day to come.[2]

Take some time to thank Jesus for giving sight to your spiritual eyes, illumination to your heart, and the longing for a new day to come.

2. Keller, in *Turning Point,* pp. 106–7.

Chapter 9

WHAT DO I HAVE
TO DO WITH YOU?

John 2:1–11

Histoy is full of great mothers who raised great children.

Modern history gives us Sandra Day O'Connor. She was born in a hospital two hundred miles from the four-room adobe house she grew up in, a house with no running water or electricity. Her mother began schooling her at home, subscribing to metropolitan newspapers as well as *New Yorker* and *Vogue* magazines so that she would learn of the rest of the world. Her mother later made sure that Sandra went to the best boarding schools possible. Before she went to college, her family visited every state capitol west of the Mississippi. Though isolated from most advantages of society, her mother made sure her daughter was prepared for whatever she wanted to do— which, as it turned out, was to be the first woman to serve on the U.S. Supreme Court.

O. J. Simpson could tell you about a special mother too. As a little boy, he suffered from rickets. There was no money for treatment, so his mother improvised a brace and corrected his problem herself. She stuck by him and kept believing in him throughout his difficult teen years. And by the time he was out of high school, he had developed the incredible athletic abilities that would make a place for him in the world—both as a professional running back in the NFL and as a public broadcaster.

Stepping back in time, there was Susanna Wesley, who had over a dozen children. But amidst the mountains of diapers and the valleys of sibling squabbles, she found time to invest in the spiritual lives of those children—which resulted in thousands of hymns from son Charles and the start of the Methodist movement from son John.

The Bible tells the stories of some great mothers too. Remember Jochebed? You might have forgotten her name, but not her son— Moses. As a baby, his life was threatened, so she hid him in a little basket among the reeds of the Nile. Later on, she worked out a plan so that she could keep him until he was weaned. His godly roots stayed with him all his life.

Then there was Samuel's mother, Hannah, who promised her son to the Lord. When he reached the age she and the Lord had agreed on, she took him to Eli the priest to be trained in spiritual things . . . and though she saw him only rarely after that, she never went back on her promise.

In the New Testament, we learn of Timothy's mother, who was the first to shape his thinking and drop the seeds of faith into his soul. And we read of Elizabeth, the mother of John the Baptist. But of all the mothers of all time, and of all the children ever conceived, none are more unique than Mary and her son Jesus. Theirs is the mother-and-child relationship we want to look at today, the one we want to study as an example for our own lives.

Jesus' Mother and Her Unique Child

Between mothers and their children there exists a universal bond that is like no other in the world—a bond of love and nurturing and responsibility. But think of the bond that Mary must have felt with this special firstborn child, a child she knew would be different from any other.

The story is as familiar to us as Dickens' *A Christmas Carol.* But in its familiarity, has it lost some of its wonder? Let's take an out-of-season look to see if we can recapture some of the emotion lost through the passage of time.

Conception and Birth

Let's start, not in a Bethlehem stable, but in the little village of Nazareth, where a young girl is startled, to say the least, by a visit from the angel Gabriel. The news he brings is even more astonishing than his presence.

> "Do not be afraid, Mary; for you have found favor with God. And behold, you will conceive in your womb, and bear a son, and you shall name Him Jesus. He will be great, and will be called the Son of the Most High; and the Lord God will give Him the throne of His father David; and He will reign over the house of Jacob forever; and His kingdom will have no end." (Luke 1:30–33)

We know the words of this message so well that we almost don't need to read them. But to Mary, they were brand new. Just imagine —she couldn't have been more than twenty years old. She had never known a man intimately, and though she was engaged to Joseph, she was not yet married. She had deliberately kept herself pure and her reputation unsullied . . . yet she was about to become an unwed teenage mother.

There can be little wonder that Joseph struggled with the news of her pregnancy. It would take an angelic visitation for most of us to believe her story too! Joseph's eventual support of her condition must have meant the world to her, but even he couldn't share the experience of a baby growing in her womb.

A mother knows the instinctive protectiveness that doesn't wait for birth—the evaluation of every bite of food, the eager gulping of extra milk, the shielding of the womb from bumps and falls. But with every flutter of movement, every prodding of tiny legs and arms, Mary knew this wasn't just any baby. It was holiness coming into the world. The responsibility must have felt overwhelming, long before that uncomfortable night in the stable.

> And she gave birth to her first-born son; and she wrapped Him in cloths, and laid Him in a manger, because there was no room for them in the inn. (2:7)

No doctors with white coats. No nurses with monitors. Not even an experienced midwife. Just a young couple who knew nothing about childbirth, and a conglomeration of the most unlikely visitors a new baby ever had—angels, shepherds, wise men, goats. But instead of sending out birth announcements to the world, Mary "treasured up all these things, pondering them in her heart" (v. 19). And the bond with her son drew tighter.

Childhood and Growth

Jesus' first twelve years are summed up in two verses.

> And when they had performed everything according to the Law of the Lord, they returned to Galilee, to their own city of Nazareth. And the Child continued to grow and become strong, increasing in wisdom; and the grace of God was upon Him. (vv. 39–40)

The next thing we know, Jesus is a preteen. Granted, He's not your typical preteen, but we see Him doing one thing that is typical —correcting His mother, albeit gently.

The family had been in Jerusalem for the Feast of the Passover. The parents had somehow become separated from Jesus, who was in the temple amazing the teachers with His spiritual insight. Understandably, they are worried when they get partway home and realize He's not with the caravan. Mary's first response, when she finds her son, is to chide Him.

"Son, why have You treated us this way? Behold, Your father and I have been anxiously looking for You." (v. 48b)

Notice the different emphasis of Jesus' words.

"Why is it that you were looking for Me? Did you not know that I had to be in My Father's house?" (v. 49)

Mary spoke of Joseph as Jesus' father; Jesus recognized His Father in heaven. As wonderful a mother as she was, she hadn't quite grasped the full scope of His mission. It hadn't quite dawned on her or on Joseph.

And they did not understand the statement which He had made to them. (v. 50)

There's a veil of silence over Jesus' teen years and His twenties. But that little incident in the temple sets us up to understand the next vignette we'll read about Jesus' life.

Adulthood and Ministry

With the passing of only a small bit of space on the page, Jesus moved from His father's carpenter shop to the Jordan River, where He emerged soaking wet from His baptism. He left home at age thirty, traveling to Jerusalem, experiencing temptation in the wilderness, choosing disciples—all well-known activities to us, but there is no conversation recorded in which He explains to His mother this transition into ministry. We know the story beginning to end, but Mary must have been somewhat in the dark. When Jesus showed up at a wedding in Cana, what she saw was not mainly the man of the great mission, but simply her oldest boy come home, the one she had leaned on all those years. Unaware of the change, or perhaps not ready for it, she behaved as any mother would. For her, the tight bond established in His childhood had not yet been loosened; the apron strings were still tightly tied.

Mary and Jesus: A Change in Relationship

As with most mothers, Mary's realization of Jesus' new identity as a grown man with His own agenda came suddenly, shockingly. And it happened at a wedding that, like so many weddings, had a last-minute crisis.

Weddings in those days were much bigger affairs than they are today. Sometimes the celebration went on for a week or more. There would be entertainment, singing, dancing, the enjoyment of food, and the flow of good wine. This wedding was no different, except that at this wedding, the hosts ran out of wine. Look at how Mary responded.

> And when the wine gave out, the mother of Jesus said to Him, "They have no wine." (John 2:3)

Sounds like an innocuous little comment. But picture your mother saying, just before the Thanksgiving meal, "There's no turkey." She wouldn't be simply stating a fact; she'd be giving a veiled command. The implication is, "Go get one!" Mary had made this kind of comment for thirty years, and it's the kind of comment you make to a boy, not a man. The relationship hadn't quite grown up with the boy; the release of the man wasn't quite complete. And Jesus didn't let this one slide by.

> "Woman, what do I have to do with you? My hour has not yet come." (v. 4)

Woman here isn't a word of insult or rebuke; it's a proper word, more like *lady*. But for all its respectfulness, there's distance in the term. What He's really saying is "Mary, what authority do you have over Me any longer?"

Mary needed to grow up as a mother. She needed to release Jesus from her authority and let Him bow to the authority of a higher power. She didn't respond angrily or defensively, but humbly acknowledged the shift of control as she passed the baton to her son.

> His mother said to the servants, "Whatever He says to you, do it." (v. 5)

Lessons for Today from Mary and Her Son

Of all the things a mother gives her children, one of the most important and most often neglected is the release of control. It's probably the hardest thing a mother can ever do. We've seen Mary struggle with this process of release; now let's look at some principles that will help us, like her, bow quietly to the necessity of it.

First: *Recognize that your child is on temporary loan, not permanent ownership.* You've considered this principle when it comes to finances and possessions; now think of it in regard to your child.

Second: *Release your child slowly and consistently, not suddenly.* It's like letting out the string on a kite—you unroll the spool a little on his first day of school, a little more when she begins to date, a little more when he begins to drive. As you release that string more and more, the wind catches the kite and you let it go until it's so small it's dancing in the sky by itself, untethered.

Don't keep such a tight grip on that ball of string that it takes a tornado to tear it out of your hands. Chances are, both you and the kite would be hurt in the process.

Third: *Realize your role is changing from director and protector to listener and friend.* When you sense a separation between you and your child, when his or her friends supplant your significance, remember that it's normal. It's healthy. Adjust your view of your role accordingly.

Fourth: *Respect the growth toward independence; don't resent it.* Remember the rest of Mary's story? Think of the things she had to witness—her son stripped, beaten, bloodied, even killed. Yet once she stepped away from interfering, she never stepped back in.

There are no guarantees that releasing your child will be pleasant. You may be disappointed, frustrated, heartsick. Yet there's no doubt that it's the right thing to do.

———————◆———————

Heavenly Father,

You know the agony of releasing Your Child. You sent Your Son from the perfect protection of heaven to live with fallible parents in a home on earth. You even allowed Him to die in order to fulfill His mission in life.

Thank You for Your example and for the example of Mary. Please help me release my children to find their own way, to fulfill their own purpose. I'm grateful, Father, that when I let go the kite strings, Your loving hand takes them. Amen.

 Living Insights STUDY ONE

Judith Viorst wrote a magazine article called "For Grown-ups Only"; in it, she repeated the stories that several women had told of times when they felt suddenly adult. Read over a few of them and see if you remember similar experiences.

> Jane: When I was 12, and our family took a trip from New York to Vermont, and Dad needed a road-map reader—and he picked *me*.
> Marcy: When I went away to college and, after four

months of eating junk food and never sleeping, I finally figured out that the person in charge of taking care of me was now *me*.

Valerie: When, after I'd worked for three whole years and saved a part of my salary every week, I bought a fur jacket completely paid for by *me*.[1]

When do you remember feeling suddenly grown up?

_____

_____

Imagine how your parents might have felt as they allowed you that opportunity. What emotions do you think they experienced? What thoughts went through their minds?

_____

_____

_____

_____

How did your parents handle the process of releasing you from their authority? What aspects of it were positive? Which were negative?

_____

_____

_____

_____

How would you like to approach it differently with your own children? If your children are already grown, are there still some ways in which you need to release their care to their heavenly Father?

_____

_____

_____

_____

1. Judith Viorst, "For Grown-ups Only," *Redbook*, July 1987, p. 39.

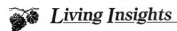

Releasing your children doesn't mean relinquishing your role as a parent; it merely means revising it. As Susanna Wesley's children left home, she committed one hour a week to praying for each of them. That may not feel as much like parenting as disciplining and instructing, but it's the most powerful kind of parenting there is.

How much time do you spend in prayer for your children? Take a few minutes right now to bring their needs before the Father, whether they are young enough to still be in your home or grown with families of their own.

Chapter 10

WHY ARE YOU REASONING IN YOUR HEARTS?

Mark 2:1–12

The greatest decision we make each day is our choice of attitude. Nothing is more important, even the circumstances that surround us.

When you stop and think about it, life can be boiled down to a simple formula: It is 10 percent what happens to us and 90 percent how we respond to it.

We waste so much time fretting over the 10 percent we can't control rather than the 90 percent that we can! We can't control the weather, flat tires, sickness, and much of the abuse we receive in life. We can, however, control our attitude toward these inclement circumstances.

No matter how rough the waters, our attitude is "the set of the sails" that directs our lives.

> One ship drives east and another drives west
>   With the selfsame winds that blow.
>   'Tis the set of the sails
>   And not the gales
>   Which tell us the way to go.
>
> Like the winds of the sea are the ways of fate,
>   As we voyage along through life:
>   'Tis the set of a soul
>   That decides its goal,
>   And not the calm or the strife.[1]

Yes, attitude is the key. "Our attitudes control our lives, attitudes are a secret power working twenty-four hours a day, for good or bad. It is of paramount importance that we know how to harness and control this great force."[2]

1. Ella Wheeler Wilcox, "The Winds of Fate," in *The Best Loved Poems of the American People,* comp. Hazel Felleman (Garden City, N.Y.: Garden City Publishing Co., 1936), p. 364.

2. Charles Simmons, as quoted in *Distilled Wisdom,* comp. and ed. Alfred Armand Montapert (Englewood Cliffs, N.J.: Prentice-Hall, 1964), p. 27.

In today's study we want to examine the crucial issue of attitude.

The All-Important Matter of Attitudes

Remember what Solomon wrote about attitudes? "As he thinketh in his heart, so is he" (Prov. 23:7).[3] A similar thought is echoed in Philippians 4:6–8.

> Be anxious for nothing, but in everything by prayer and supplication with thanksgiving let your requests be made known to God. And the peace of God, which surpasses all comprehension, shall guard your hearts and your minds in Christ Jesus.
>
> Finally, brethren, whatever is true, whatever is honorable, whatever is right, whatever is pure, whatever is lovely, whatever is of good repute, if there is any excellence and if anything worthy of praise, let your mind dwell on these things.

How our attitudes toward our circumstances would change if we took those verses to heart! And how content we would become if we developed the positive approach toward life that Paul exemplifies a little farther down in the same chapter.

> Not that I speak from want; for I have learned to be content in whatever circumstances I am. I know how to get along with humble means, and I also know how to live in prosperity; in any and every circumstance I have learned the secret of being filled and going hungry, both of having abundance and suffering need. I can do all things through Him who strengthens me. (vv. 11–13)

Paul refused to blame life for his circumstances. So should we. To blame life would be like blaming a piano for our inability to make music on it.

Another crucial concept about attitudes surfaces in the aftermath of a conflict between Jesus and the religious leaders. In a scathing criticism of their hypocrisy, Jesus rebukes them for worshiping God with their lips while their hearts are far from Him (Mark 7:6–7). Turning from the scribes and Pharisees, Jesus explains to the crowd:

> "Listen to Me, all of you, and understand: there is nothing outside the man which going into him can

3. King James Version.

defile him; but the things which proceed out of the man are what defile the man. . . . For from within, out of the heart of men, proceed the evil thoughts, fornications, thefts, murders, adulteries, deeds of coveting and wickedness, as well as deceit, sensuality, envy, slander, pride and foolishness. All these evil things proceed from within and defile the man." (vv. 14–15, 21–23)

Jesus' point? The heart—not our surrounding circumstances—is the source of our attitudes.

As we take a closer look at the list of evil things in Mark 7:21–23, we see how powerful attitudes are. Though they enter as imperceptible seeds sown in our hearts, they have latent within them an orchard of sordid fruit.

Attitudes in Contrast

Turning to Mark 2, we encounter a scene that can teach us much regarding attitudes. The stage is set in the first four verses.

And when He had come back to Capernaum several days afterward, it was heard that He was at home. And many were gathered together, so that there was no longer room, even near the door; and He was speaking the word to them. And they came, bringing to Him a paralytic, carried by four men. And being unable to get to Him because of the crowd, they removed the roof above Him; and when they had dug an opening, they let down the pallet on which the paralytic was lying. (vv. 1–4)

Word traveled quickly that Jesus was back home, and a large crowd spontaneously gathered—the house was packed to hear Him speak. The Greek word for *speak* in verse 2, though, is not the term for formal, authoritative speaking. Instead, it indicates that in this shoulder-to-shoulder setting, Jesus is talking informally about the Old Testament Scriptures. As He does, a pin-drop silence falls over the audience.

In contrast to this quiet on the inside, there is a commotion on the outside. Four men are carrying a paralyzed man on a stretcher, trying to wedge him through the wall of flesh that stands at the door, craning to catch a few of Jesus' words. Unable to make an opening, they take their handicapped friend up the outside stairs to the roof.

Homes in that region had flat roofs with either stairs or ladders on the outside wall. The roofs were composed of stone or tiles covered with dirt and seeded with grass. These men literally dug through the soil to lift the tiles away. Then they carefully lowered their friend on his padded pallet into the group around Jesus. It's a beautiful picture of faith in action. When the house was full, they took the stairs. When the roof was closed, they dug through the tiles. When distance was too great, they lowered a rope.

As these men look hopefully down from the hole in the roof, Jesus utters the words that will reveal a contrast in attitudes.

> And Jesus seeing their faith said to the paralytic, "My son, your sins are forgiven." (v. 5)

Such a statement clearly implies that Jesus was acting upon His authority to dismiss the guilt of the man's sin. It took divine insight to know that there was a greater need in the sick man's life than being healed physically.

No doubt, this man was overly sensitive to his own failures. In his day, people believed that the greater the affliction, the greater the sin. But with one sweeping statement of compassion, Jesus puts the man's haunting introspections to rest.

The attitude of the man on the pallet and his friends overhead is one of faith in Jesus' divinity. The attitude that rippled through the crowd, however, is one of unbelief.

> But there were some of the scribes sitting there and reasoning in their hearts, "Why does this man speak that way? He is blaspheming; who can forgive sins but God alone?" And immediately Jesus, aware in His spirit that they were reasoning that way within themselves, said to them, "Why are you reasoning about these things in your hearts? Which is easier, to say to the paralytic, 'Your sins are forgiven'; or to say, 'Arise, and take up your pallet and walk'?" (vv. 6–9)

Like vultures, the scribes pick apart His words, judge His motives, and criticize His theology. But Jesus isn't fooled by the crisp whiteness of their finely sewn togas. He sees beyond the exterior and into their hearts, as is evidenced by the use of the word *reasoning*, repeated three times in this passage (vv. 6, 8).

The word means "to deliberate, to turn things over in your mind, to bring together various thoughts and come to a conclusion." Jesus perceives by His spirit the cynical thoughts of these men—"Who does He think He is? *God?*"

The question Jesus poses to the scribes asks: Which is easier, to *say* something or to *prove* it? Jesus does both.

> "But in order that you may know that the Son of Man has authority on earth to forgive sins"—He said to the paralytic—"I say to you, rise, take up your pallet and go home." And he rose and immediately took up the pallet and went out in the sight of all. (vv. 10–12a)

In the wake of the miracle, the skeptics were left gaping in amazement.

> So that they were all amazed and were glorifying God, saying, "We have never seen anything like this." (v. 12b)

Matthew says they were "filled with awe" (9:8). Luke describes them as "seized with astonishment . . . filled with fear" (5:26). All three synoptic Gospel writers add that they glorified God.

Alfred Edersheim comments on the scene:

> As the healed man slowly rose, and, still silent, rolled up his pallet, a way was made for him between this multitude which followed him with wondering eyes. . . . The amazement of fear fell on them in this Presence, and they glorified God, and they said: 'We have never seen it on this wise!'[4]

Suddenly they were forced to deal with their attitude.

Dealing with Skepticism . . . Focusing on Faith

The attitudes of faith and unbelief are represented in the two groups we studied, but they're no less apparent in people today.

Is an attitude of unbelief pervading your soul, permeating it with negativism, pessimism, and criticism? Though these qualities may be hidden below the surface, they're still there, seething in the caldron of your heart.

If this attitude characterizes your inner being, Jesus wants to ask you a very pointed question: Why are you reasoning this way in your heart? Realize that if you harbor skepticism, it will poison your spirit and spill acid on your soul.

4. Alfred Edersheim, *The Life and Times of Jesus the Messiah* (Grand Rapids, Mich.: William B. Eerdmans Publishing Co., 1959), vol. 1, p. 506.

Maybe you're not one of the skeptics in the crowd. Maybe you're one of the minority who have a strong confidence in the Lord's ability to bring healing and hope. If so, are you befriending someone as helpless as that paralytic was? Are you putting a shoulder to your faith and overcoming any obstacles to bring that person to Jesus?

Remember, just as faith without works is dead, so are attitudes without actions. For without a handful of faithful friends who were willing to lift a pallet and dig through a roof, the paralytic would never have received the forgiveness or the healing he so desperately yearned for.

◆

Dear Father,

Give us the faith to lift pallets, climb stairs, dig through ceilings, and lower ropes. Help us to overcome any obstacle in order to bring our cares to You. Give us the forgiveness we need to stand tall so that we might take up our pallets and walk free. Deliver us from the cynicism of those looking on in the crowd, and from any attitude that would keep us from coming to Your feet. We pray in Jesus' name. Amen.

 Living Insights STUDY ONE

Let's take a minute for an attitude evaluation exercise.

- Is your attitude poisoning any of your relationships? How could the advice in Philippians 2:3–8 help you?

_____

_____

_____

_____

- Do you have any problems with your attitude toward your circumstances? Which of the following passages speaks most clearly to your area of need?

Matthew 6:25–34   Philippians 4:6–8
Romans 8:31–39   Philippians 4:12–13
2 Corinthians 4:8–9

- Read Job 1 and examine Job's attitude in the midst of his cata-strophic loss. Describe the outlook that sustained him during that tragic time.

_____

_____

- What kind of attitude do you think you would have if you traded places with Job?

_____

_____

_____

- The key to Job's attitude during the storms of life is found in his relationship with God when all was calm. Describe what it was like.

_____

_____

_____

Living Insights   STUDY TWO

Faith and unbelief are two distinct attitudes found in our passage about the paralytic. Look up the following four passages and suc-cinctly jot down the principles found there regarding faith.

John 20:24–29 _____

2 Corinthians 4:18 _____

2 Corinthians 5:7 _____

Hebrews 11:6 _____

Read through the account of the spies sent to report on the Promised Land in Numbers 13:1–14:35. What were the consequences of their unbelief?

_____

_____

_____

What attitude characterized the children of Israel in the wilderness (see Exod. 15:22–24, 16:1–3, 17:1–3)?

_____

What lay at the root of that attitude (see Heb. 3:7–19)?

_____

If this is a problem in your life, what can you do to uproot it (see Rom. 10:17)?

_____

Chapter 11

WHAT IS THAT TO YOU?

John 21:15–22

Of the many scenes captured on the pages of the Gospel accounts, none is more intimate than the one portrayed in John 21. Jesus and His men are together at the shoreline. His disciples have eaten breakfast and are resting on the sand after an all-night fishing trip. No doubt, small talk and quiet dialogues fill the air as the final embers of the fire burn out. Then an unforgettable conversation between Peter and the Lord begins. As the penetrating words of Jesus reach a climax, He gives the disciple a clear command— "Follow Me!"

What occurs after that causes Jesus to ask another of His probing questions, one that still carries with it a relevant and inescapable message. If you happen to be one of those people who pays closer attention to others' lives than to your own need for obedience . . . listen up!

A Question You May Find Hard to Answer

When was the last time someone should have told you to mind your own business? Perhaps it was when you hastily jumped to a conclusion regarding someone else's mistakes. Maybe it was when you band-aided a pious platitude over someone else's pain. Or possibly it was when, uninvited and ill-informed, you proceeded to stick your nose into someone else's affairs.

The real question is—if we can be blunt—Are you the nosy type? Pretty bold question. But with busybodies,[1] subtlety is not the best policy—honesty is. If you think that question is confrontational, take a look at the way Jesus and His contemporaries squared off on the issue. Jesus said:

> "Don't criticise people, and you will not be criticised. For you will be judged by the way you criticise others, and the measure you give will be the measure you receive.
> "Why do you look at the speck of sawdust in your brother's eye and fail to notice the plank in your own?

---

1. Interestingly, the two times the word *busybody* is used in the New Testament, it is connected with idleness (see 2 Thess. 3:11, 1 Tim. 5:13).

How can you say to your brother, 'Let me get the speck out of your eye', when there is a plank in your own? You fraud! Take the plank out of your own eye first, and then you can see clearly enough to remove your brother's speck of dust." (Matt. 7:1–5)[2]

Paul was equally forceful:

Each of us must bear some faults and burdens of his own. For none of us is perfect! (Gal. 6:5)[3]

None of you should think only of his own affairs, but should learn to see things from other people's point of view. (Phil. 2:4)[4]

James is even more forthright:

The human tongue is physically small, but what tremendous effects it can boast of! A whole forest can be set ablaze by a tiny spark of fire, and the tongue is as dangerous as any fire, with vast potentialities for evil. It can poison the whole body, it can make the whole of life a blazing hell. (James 3:5–6)[5]

And Peter adds:

Don't let me hear of your suffering for murdering or stealing or making trouble or being a busybody and prying into other people's affairs. (1 Pet. 4:15)[6]

In the previous study, we talked about the value of maintaining the right *attitude*. Today, we want to examine the value of the right *perspective*, the value of not judging others prematurely. Giving people room to decide for themselves, to differ from the crowd, to walk to the beat of a different drummer.

In order for that to happen, we must allow the Spirit of God to deliver us from comparison. Remember, each of us must stand before the judgment seat of Christ. And when we do, we will never be asked to account for another person's life—only our own (2 Cor. 5:10).

2. J. B. Phillips, The New Testament in Modern English (London, England: Geoffrey Bles, 1960).

3. The Living Bible (Wheaton, Ill.: Tyndale House Publishers, 1971).

4. Phillips, The New Testament in Modern English.

5. Phillips, The New Testament in Modern English.

6. The Living Bible.

A Command Anyone Could Understand

In case the sweat of incrimination is beading on your hairline, let's change the subject from a hard-to-answer question to a command anyone could understand.

The setting for Jesus' command in John 21 is an idyllic shore on Galilee's sea. The rhythm of the lapping waves creates a mood of tranquility, and the smell of broiled fish curls warmly through the morning chill. Breakfast is served from the nail-scarred hands of the resurrected Christ. The disciples take the fish with a certain measure of reserve.

A reverent hush falls over the group like an incoming fog as the very one who would most prefer blending into the scenery is suddenly brought center stage.

That person is Peter. He was the former spokesman for the group, the ardent loyalist, the impulsive, outspoken brother of Andrew. Now he sits with the other disciples around the campfire. He sits despondently, a broken man, a man who desperately needs to be reinstated.

> So when they had finished breakfast, Jesus said to Simon Peter, "Simon, son of John, do you love Me more than these?" (v. 15a)

Notice that Jesus doesn't call him Peter, which means "rock." He calls him Simon, the name he was known by before Jesus came into his life. At his lowest ebb, Peter had blurted out, "I do not know Him who is called the Christ." And he's been carrying that guilt on his back ever since.

Now the One who was denied looks him in the eyes to plumb the depths of his devotion—"Do you love Me more than these?" It is an embarrassing moment as the other disciples look on. James and John included. Along with Peter, these two were the most intimate of Jesus' confidants. They formed the inner circle. They were together at the high point on the Mount of Transfiguration and at the low point in the Garden of Gethsemane.

John had heard Peter announce in the Upper Room that "even though all may fall away because of You, I will never fall away" (Matt. 26:33).

There was an edge of competition that cut into all the disciples' relationships with each other. More than once they had argued over who would be greatest in the kingdom (Mark 9:34; Luke 9:46, 22:24). Undoubtedly, there was also a tendency on the part of even those closest to Jesus to compare themselves to each other. We will see that as we continue in the John 21 passage.

Three times Jesus asks Peter if he loves Him—once for each time Peter had denied Him.

> [Peter] said to Him, "Yes, Lord; You know that I love You." He said to him, "Tend My lambs." He said to him again a second time, "Simon, son of John, do you love Me?" He said to Him, "Yes, Lord; You know that I love You." He said to him, "Shepherd My sheep." He said to him the third time, "Simon, son of John, do you love Me?" Peter was grieved because He said to him the third time, "Do you love Me?" And he said to Him, "Lord, You know all things; You know that I love You." Jesus said to him, "Tend My sheep." (vv. 15b–17)

Those words of affirmation must have meant so much to Peter. They meant "I forgive you . . . I still love you . . . I still believe you're the right man for the job." As the others watched and listened, Jesus reinstated Peter and challenged him to return with fresh vigor to the calling of God on his life.

After those warming words, Jesus utters a chilling prophecy.

> "Truly, truly, I say to you, when you were younger, you used to gird yourself, and walk wherever you wished; but when you grow old, you will stretch out your hands, and someone else will gird you, and bring you where you do not wish to go." (v. 18)

The mysterious words are clarified parenthetically in verse 19 and are followed by a command that would take Peter to a new plateau of commitment.

> Now this He said, signifying by what kind of death he would glorify God. And when He had spoken this, He said to him, "Follow Me!" (v. 19)

With the words "follow Me," the restoration is complete. And as a result of those words, Peter's life would become a tangible illustration of Matthew 10:38—"He who does not take his cross and follow after Me is not worthy of Me."[7]

---

7. According to Jerome, Peter was eventually crucified, but upside down, since he considered himself unworthy to die in the same manner as Christ. See *Fox's Book of Martyrs,* ed. William Byron Forbush (New York, N.Y.: Holt, Rinehart and Winston, 1954; reprint, Grand Rapids, Mich.: Zondervan Publishing House, 1967), p. 4.

A Response Many Would Have Given

With his life dangling in the balance, Peter takes a minute to consider the call. Understandably, he hesitates. And he falls back into a pattern that has been so prevalent among the disciples over the past few years—comparison.

> Peter, turning around, saw the disciple whom Jesus loved following them; the one who also had leaned back on His breast at the supper, and said, "Lord, who is the one who betrays You?" Peter therefore seeing him said to Jesus, "Lord, and what about this man?" (John 21:20–21)

The question is asked almost with a tinge of resentment—"After all, Lord, is it really fair to make such demands on me and not on John?"

His is a response many would have given, but Jesus meets it with a swift rebuke.

> "If I want him to remain until I come, what is that to you? You follow Me!" (v. 22)

A. B. Bruce, in his fine work *The Training of the Twelve*, writes insightfully:

> Jesus replies to him as if he were a busybody, meddling with matters with which he had no concern. And, indeed, busybodyism was one of Peter's faults. He was fond of looking after and managing other people; he tried once and again to manage the Lord Himself. Curiously enough, it is from this apostle that the Church gets the needful warning against the too common vice just named. "Let none of you," he writes in his first epistle, "suffer as a murderer, or as a thief, or as an evil-doer, or *as a busybody in other men's matters.*"[8]

At the root of Peter's question is envy of the worst kind. And how many times has Jesus' rebuke been the one *we* have needed to hear when we started comparing ourselves to others!

"Lord, I'm driving this old rattletrap and look at the new car he's driving."

"What is that to you?"

---

8. A. B. Bruce, *The Training of the Twelve* (Grand Rapids, Mich.: Kregel Publications, 1971), pp. 527–28.

"Lord, I'm living for You and just barely getting by, while our friends are living for themselves and enjoying 'the good life.'"

"What is that to you?"

"Lord, I'm being faithful and struggling to hold my marriage together, while the person I work with is divorced and doing great."

"What is that to you?"

A Lesson All Should Learn

God's calling is personal and His leading is unique. Although the message of salvation is as narrow as the cross of Christ, His individual will for His children is as broad as the grace of God.

All Christians enroll in the same school, but our individual curricula is vastly different. Because we have different needs, different gifts, and different callings, our course work is tailor-made to match. We are not cookie-cutter Christians. Although we're cut out of the same dough, we are not cut out in the same size or shape as even our closest friends or coworkers.

We are all predestined to become like Christ (Rom. 8:29). The route God takes us to get there, however, varies significantly from one person to another.

———◆———

Our Father,

> *We ask You for a special measure of courage to address this question Your Son asked. We pray that—as You minister to every one of us in a particular way, saying one thing to one person and something altogether different to another—we would not look around at everyone else, but follow You with a singleness of eye.*

> *But mainly, our Father, we pray that we might be people with broad shoulders and understanding spirits, not compromising one whit on the truth and principles of Scripture, but giving people room to be and to grow and to serve as You lead them. May we respect their walk as deeply as we are committed to our own. We pray in the name of Christ our Savior. Amen.*

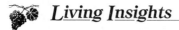

We've taken a good look at Peter's problem with comparison; now let's examine our own lives for traces of that crippling quality.

As you see others receive the things you want, how do you respond inwardly? Are you like a whining child demanding equal treatment? Do you grumble under your breath about the unfairness of it all? Or do you gratefully accept the position God has allowed you to be in at this time? Honestly describe your typical reaction.

_____

_____

_____

It's difficult to see God's generosity toward us when our attention is fixed on the things we've been denied. And it's defeating to try to follow His plan while kicking against it at the same time. Read Romans 9:20–21. From this passage, and from what you've learned in this study, jot down one or two principles that will help keep your eyes on your Father and your nose out of other people's business.

_____

_____

_____

_____

_____

 Living Insights   STUDY TWO

Busybodyness comes in lots of forms. Comparing God's plan for you to God's plan for your neighbor is only one of them. Another comes into focus in Matthew 7:3–4.

> "Why do you look at the speck of sawdust in your brother's eye and fail to notice the plank in your own? How can you say to your brother, 'Let me get the speck out of your eye', when there is a plank in your own?"[9]

9. Phillips, The New Testament in Modern English.

Who of us hasn't been guilty of justifying our faults while criticizing those of others! What flaw in others have you found yourself nitpicking lately?

_____

_____

_____

_____

_____

Your annoyance at that flaw may or may not be justified. But for now, let's skip over the specks in other people's eyes and focus on our own. If an ophthalmologist was shining a light into your eye, would any planks be found sticking out? Before you criticize someone else's irresponsible spending, you might want to look closer at past purchases of your own. Before you get picky about the offensive behavior of others, evaluate the way _you_ come across. Write down any sheepish admissions that come to mind. As you do, thank God for His gracious forgiveness and endless patience with your rationalized human mistakes.

_____

_____

_____

_____

_____

_____

_____

Chapter 12

ARE YOU THE TEACHER . . . AND DO NOT UNDERSTAND?

John 3:1–18

Anyone who speaks openly of Christ soon discovers an interesting contrast. Many people are genuinely interested, open, and receptive. Some, however, are closed and defensive when the subject of salvation comes up, even though they may be churchgoers.

Why such a difference? The primary reason is a difference in philosophies. Those who place their faith in external good works to gain God's favor could be described as having a *humanistic religion*. Its emphasis on human accomplishment can span the spectrum from grand philanthropic gestures to something as simple as regular Sunday school attendance.

A diametrically opposed philosophy is that of *divine regeneration*. In this way of believing, the basis of acceptance from God is not in climbing a ladder of good works; rather, it's in acknowledging the fact that we are sinners, incapable of pleasing Him in our unregenerate state. Salvation comes only as an undeserved gift of God. The emphasis, then, shifts from one of human accomplishment to one of God's grace.

For some, that's a pretty hard concept to swallow. And sometimes it seems that the more religious people are, the more they choke on the thought.

Today we are going to see Jesus confront a religious teacher who held a humanistic philosophy. The dialogue that emerges from the discussion proves to be one of the most poignant in all of Scripture.

Unexpected Conversation: A Pharisee and Jesus

The clandestine encounter is found in John 3.

> Now there was a man of the Pharisees, named Nicodemus, a ruler of the Jews; this man came to Him by night, and said to Him, "Rabbi, we know that You have come from God as a teacher; for no one can do these signs that You do unless God is with him." (vv. 1–2)

92

From these verses we find out two things about Nicodemus—he was a Pharisee and a ruler of the Jews. If we look down to verse 10, we also learn that he was a teacher of Israel. William Barclay provides some important background regarding this prominent religious leader.

> Nicodemus was a Pharisee. In many ways the Pharisees were the best people in the whole country. There were never more than 6,000 of them; they were what was known as a *chaburah*, or brotherhood. They entered into this brotherhood by taking a pledge in front of three witnesses that they would spend all their lives observing every detail of the scribal law.[1]

The passage tells us that Nicodemus initiated the meeting. He came to Jesus, not the other way around. And surprisingly, he came as a seeker of truth, not as an adversary brandishing some theological sword.

There's one other thing we learn from the passage. He came at night.

> *At night.*
> Two words between the lines in his resume that follow him through the Gospel like a stray. When John later describes him, he doesn't mention the credentials but rather this telling clue to his character: "Nicodemus, the man who earlier had visited Jesus *at night.*"
> Thus, cloaked in darkness, Nicodemus wends his way through the side streets of Jerusalem . . . slowly . . . cautiously . . . every so often stepping into the shadows to avoid recognition.
> He comes as a seeker of truth. But he comes at night.
> He comes not in an official capacity but in a personal one. It is a chancy meeting. Gossip could hurt him. He has much to lose—his prestige as Israel's teacher, his position on the ruling council, his entire peer group.[2]

Nicodemus comes with questions, questions that have probably kept him up nights as his conscience tossed and turned. *Could the*

1. William Barclay, *The Gospel of John*, rev. ed., The Daily Study Bible Series (Philadelphia, Pa.: Westminster Press, 1975), vol. 1, p. 120.

2. Ken Gire, *Intimate Moments with the Savior* (Grand Rapids, Mich.: Zondervan Publishing House, Daybreak Books, 1989), pp. 12–13.

miracles possibly be genuine? Could the whispered rumors be true? Could this man be the Messiah?

So he who is the teacher of Israel comes with a notepad full of questions, a sharp pencil, and a searching heart.

> "Rabbi, we know that You have come from God as a teacher; for no one can do these signs that You do unless God is with him." Jesus answered and said to him, "Truly, truly, I say to you, unless one is born again, he cannot see the kingdom of God." (vv. 2b–3)

Christ's reply is terse and to the point. He cuts through the protocol and, with rapier precision, opens the man's heart to the stringent realities of God's kingdom. Jesus' meaning? Just as physical birth from our mother's womb ushers us into the physical world, so spiritual birth is necessary to bring us into the spiritual world (see 1:12–13).

Underscore the word *cannot* in 3:3. It implies incapability rather than prohibition. Just as a tadpole is incapable of leaving the world of water to live in the world of air, so the natural man is incapable of entering the spiritual kingdom. Unless a metamorphosis takes place. And that's the point of the "born again" metaphor.

Nicodemus, however, misses the point, interpreting the figurative image in a literal way.

> Nicodemus said to Him, "How can a man be born when he is old? He cannot enter a second time into his mother's womb and be born, can he?" (v. 4)

His interest is piqued, but he is confused—the typical reaction of a natural man (see 1 Cor. 2:14). Patiently, Jesus tries to unravel the mystery in terms Nicodemus will understand.

> Jesus answered, "Truly, truly, I say to you, unless one is born of water and the Spirit, he cannot enter into the kingdom of God. That which is born of the flesh is flesh, and that which is born of the Spirit is spirit. Do not marvel that I said to you, 'You must be born again.' The wind blows where it wishes and you hear the sound of it, but do not know where it comes from and where it is going; so is everyone who is born of the Spirit." (John 3:5–8)

Jesus explains that one must be born of "water and the Spirit." To a Pharisee, water was associated with cleansing, since it was used in the numerous ceremonial rites of cleansing. The content and construction of the sentence in Greek suggests that the "and" linking *water* and *Spirit* should be translated "even":[3] "unless one is born of water, even the Spirit, he cannot enter into the kingdom of God." In other words, Jesus is saying that in order to be born again there must be an inward cleansing brought about by the Holy Spirit.

Jesus then gives two illustrations you would think even a child could understand—one of physical birth (vv. 6–7) and one of the presence of wind (v. 8). But by now Nicodemus is scratching his head.

> Nicodemus answered and said to Him, "How can these things be?" (v. 9)

Jesus returns the question with a penetrating one of His own.

> Jesus answered and said to him, "Are you the teacher of Israel, and do not understand these things?"[4] (v. 10)

Jesus lays His cards on the table: "Look, Nicodemus, if you can't understand 'See Spot run,' why should I introduce you to Shakespeare?"

> "Truly, truly, I say to you, we speak that which we know, and bear witness of that which we have seen; and you do not receive our witness. If I told you earthly things and you do not believe, how shall you believe if I tell you heavenly things?" (vv. 11–12)

But instead of giving up on the bewildered student, Jesus picks an illustration that Nicodemus might understand—one from the Old Testament.

> "And as Moses lifted up the serpent in the wilderness, even so must the Son of Man be lifted up; that whoever believes may in Him have eternal life." (vv. 14–15)

The key to the historical picture is found in the words "even so." The comparison is crucial, for Jesus was not giving a history lesson about snakes but an illustration about salvation. In Numbers 21:4–9 God provided deliverance in the wilderness from the bite of the fiery

---

3. For a similar construction, see Titus 3:5 where "the washing of regeneration" is equivalent to, rather than coordinate to, the "renewing by the Holy Spirit." For an Old Testament parallel that juxtaposed the water and the Spirit, see Ezekiel 36:25–27.

4. The presence of the definite article does not mean Nicodemus was the *only* teacher in Israel; it is merely a reference to his being well-known and respected.

serpents sent as a judgment upon the grumbling Israelites. All the bitten Israelites had to do to be healed was look at the bronze serpent that Moses lifted up. They didn't have to do good works as penance or go through any religious ritual for cleansing.

All they had to do was believe, with just a simple look of faith. In the same way, all we have to do is look to the Cross in faith, God's provision for all who are in a wilderness of sin.

Essential Clarification

Three issues are at stake in Jesus' conversation with Nicodemus. One has to do with *response.* There are only two ways we can respond to what Jesus has said—in belief or in unbelief.

> "For God so loved the world, that He gave His only begotten Son, that whoever believes in Him should not perish, but have eternal life." (John 3:16)

The second issue that hangs in the balance has to do with *destiny.* Again, there are only two alternatives—eternal life or eternal death, salvation or judgment, deliverance or destruction.

> "For God did not send the Son into the world to judge the world, but that the world should be saved through Him. He who believes in Him is not judged; he who does not believe has been judged already, because he has not believed in the name of the only begotten Son of God." (vv. 17–18)

The final issue of importance relates to *choice.* We must either receive the gift God offers or reject it. There is no middle road on the highway to heaven. Jesus is the only way (14:6). Like Nicodemus, we can either take a step of faith to follow Him or turn and walk away.

> A lifetime of studying and teaching the Word, and now Nicodemus is face to face with the Word incarnate.
>
> He came in darkness. Now he stands in the glowing presence of the Light of the World. He is a short step from the kingdom of God, at the very gate. And as the fluid words cascade from Jesus' lips, he realizes— this is he of whom the prophets spoke.
>
> A spark touches the far edges of his soul, but it is a slow burn. For Nicodemus is a careful man. And he has much to lose.
>
> Still, an ember has fallen into his heart. An ember that tragedy will someday fan to a blaze of courage. And it will be this tragedy that brings Nicodemus out

of the shadows to the side of the Savior . . . in the full light of day.[5]

Nicodemus chose to follow. When, we don't know. Or where. But in John 7:44–52, he makes a defense on Jesus' behalf. Then, when Jesus is crucified, Nicodemus finally steps from the shadows with Joseph of Arimathea to make sure the Savior has a respectable burial.

Even though Jesus' words may not have brought about an immediate metamorphosis in Nicodemus that bewildering night, they eventually did their work.

◆

Dear Father,

We thank You for giving us a Book of Truth. Thank You for communicating in terms we can understand.

And now, our Father, as we act upon what we have heard, give us courage like that of Nicodemus to come out of the shadows, to look You right square in the eye and confess our need and be willing to go to whatever lengths are needed for You and for Your cause.

Unto Him who is able to guard us from stumbling and present us faultless before the presence of His glory with exceeding joy, to the only wise God our Savior, be glory and majesty, dominion and power, both now and forever. Amen.

 Living Insights STUDY ONE

If Nicodemus were faced with the assignment of writing his testimony, surely he would point back to that fateful night when Jesus turned his whole world upside down.

Reflect on your own conversion, and on the following page explain how you came to be born again. First, tell what led to your conversion, then describe your spiritual birth, and finally, conclude with a description of your subsequent growth as a Christian.

5. Gire, *Intimate Moments with the Savior,* p. 15.

Events that led to my spiritual birth: _____

_____

_____

_____

_____

_____

_____

_____

The birth itself: _____

_____

_____

_____

_____

_____

_____

_____

My growth since becoming a Christian: _____

_____

_____

_____

_____

_____

_____

_____

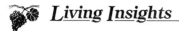 **_Living Insights_**

Nicodemus was confronted with some pretty revolutionary ideas when he met with Jesus. Undoubtedly, he got little sleep as he wrestled with the questions Jesus threw at him that night.

Is there a nagging question that you have for Jesus? Something that's eating away at you and won't let you rest?

Or maybe there is a question Jesus has thrown your way, a question that has snagged your heart like a fish hook . . . a painful question, one that hurts just to think about. If so, remember, He's not there to hurt you but to draw you to Himself.

Bring those barbed questions to Him, won't you? Maybe His inviting words in Matthew 11:28–29 will make it easier.

> "Come to Me, all who are weary and heavy-laden, and I will give you rest. Take My yoke upon you, and learn from Me, for I am gentle and humble in heart; and you shall find rest for your souls."

Take some time now to bring those things to the Lord in prayer.

Chapter 13

THE CUP WHICH THE FATHER HAS GIVEN ... SHALL I NOT DRINK IT?

John 18:1–11

Suffering is a hard cup to drink from. Especially when you live in a society, as we do, that is governed by the pleasure principle. We go to extravagant means to find pleasure, and if it is beyond our reach, we search for something—anything—to numb our pain.

But where we push away the bitter cup of suffering, Jesus raised that chalice to His lips. Those who follow Christ soon learn that there is no escaping that cup. To Him, it meant anguish, humiliation, and the pain of crucifixion. To us, it may mean many things, all of them difficult; some, even excruciating.

The question Jesus posed to Peter—"The cup which the Father has given Me, shall I not drink it?"—raises a crucial issue. It forces us to think, challenges us to submit, and bids us to take and drink the cup God has placed before *us.*

On Being a Christian and Becoming a Disciple

Suffering is an important course in discipleship. But before we look at the syllabus for Suffering 101, it's important to note that it's a graduate course in the Christian life. For just as there is a difference between an incoming freshman and a graduate student, so there is a difference between being a Christian and becoming a disciple.

Christianity is based on another's sacrifice; discipleship, however, is based on our own. Jesus outlines the course in Luke 9:23.

> And He was saying to them all, "If anyone wishes to come after Me, let him deny himself, and take up his cross daily, and follow Me."

From this passage we can derive a fairly accurate definition of a disciple: *A believer whose commitment to Christ has grown into a deep desire to obey, regardless of the outcome or consequences.*

Jesus lists three specifics.

First: *The disciple must "deny himself."* Literally, it means "to say no to, to refuse to acknowledge." The verb is sometimes even rendered "disown." To enthrone God we must dethrone self if we are ever to make Him the ruling passion of our life.

Second: *The disciple must "take up his cross daily."* The cross is a symbol of death. Spiritually, it represents a deliberate decision to abandon one's own desires, preferences, and plans—and to live with the consequences of that decision, regardless of how painful they are.

Third: *The disciple must "follow Me."* Just as a child mimics behavior in the game "Follow the Leader," so the disciple must mimic the behavior of Christ, following Him to the ends of the earth . . . and, if necessary, even to Calvary.

Jesus Christ: The Perfect Example

As we turn to John 18, we find Jesus' disciples following Him faithfully right up to the time of His arrest. The setting is sober. Their last meal together has ended. And so has the Upper Room Discourse. Jesus' prayer to the Father has also concluded. Now He and His eleven faithful followers are making their way to the Garden of Gethsemane, where the Savior will make a final plea to the Father for "the cup" to be taken from Him.

> When Jesus had spoken these words, He went forth with His disciples over the ravine of the Kidron, where there was a garden, into which He Himself entered, and His disciples. (John 18:1)

William Barclay describes their descent into the ravine.

> They would leave by the gate, go down the steep valley and cross the channel of the brook Kedron [*sic*]. There a symbolic thing must have happened. All the Passover lambs were killed in the Temple, and the blood of the lambs was poured on the altar as an offering to God. The number of lambs slain for the Passover was immense. On one occasion, thirty years later than the time of Jesus, a census was taken and the number was 256,000. We may imagine what the Temple courts were like when the blood of all these lambs was dashed on to the altar. From the altar there was a channel down to the brook Kedron, and through the channel the blood of the Passover lambs drained away. When Jesus

crossed the brook Kedron it would still be red with the blood of the lambs which had been sacrificed.[1]

Crossing the Kidron, Jesus comes to Gethsemane. He comes to pray.

> Then Jesus came with them to a place called Geth-semane, and said to His disciples, "Sit here while I go over there and pray." And He took with Him Peter and the two sons of Zebedee, and began to be grieved and distressed. Then He said to them, "My soul is deeply grieved, to the point of death; remain here and keep watch with Me." And He went a little beyond them, and fell on His face and prayed, saying, "My Father, if it is possible, let this cup pass from Me; yet not as I will, but as Thou wilt." And He came to the disciples and found them sleeping, and said to Peter, "So, you men could not keep watch with Me for one hour? Keep watching and praying, that you may not enter into temptation; the spirit is willing, but the flesh is weak." He went away again a second time and prayed, saying, "My Father, if this cannot pass away unless I drink it, Thy will be done." And again He came and found them sleeping, for their eyes were heavy. And He left them again, and went away and prayed a third time, saying the same thing once more. (Matt. 26:36–44)

A. T. Robertson comments:

> *This cup.* . . . The figure can mean only the approach-ing death. . . . The Master is about to taste the bitter dregs in the cup of death for the sin of the world.[2]

Into the middle of all this passion and pathos, Judas leads a torchlit crowd.

> Now Judas also, who was betraying Him, knew the place; for Jesus had often met there with His disciples. Judas then, having received the Roman cohort, and officers from the chief priests and the Pharisees, came there with lanterns and torches and weapons. (John 18:2–3)

1. William Barclay, *The Gospel of John*, rev. ed., The Daily Study Bible Series (Phila-delphia, Pa.: Westminster Press, 1975), vol. 2, p. 221.

2. A. T. Robertson, *Word Pictures in the New Testament* (Nashville, Tenn.: Broadman Press, 1930), vol. 1, pp. 212–13.

The crowd came armed for a fight, but they were in for a disarming surprise.

A Surprising Surrender

As we read the account in verses 4–9, one element is conspicuous by its absence. There is no resistance on the part of Jesus. No impulse to run and hide. Not even a trace of reluctance.

> Jesus therefore, knowing all the things that were coming upon Him, went forth, and said to them, "Whom do you seek?" They answered Him, "Jesus the Nazarene." He said to them, "I am He." And Judas also who was betraying Him, was standing with them. When therefore He said to them, "I am He," they drew back, and fell to the ground. Again therefore He asked them, "Whom do you seek?" And they said, "Jesus the Nazarene." Jesus answered, "I told you that I am He; if therefore you seek Me, let these go their way," that the word might be fulfilled which He spoke, "Of those whom Thou hast given Me I lost not one."

Why is the Savior so full of surrender? Because He had fought His battle already, in the garden. Now He is merely extending His hand to take the cup which the Father has prepared for Him.

A Typical Reaction

Peter had vowed to stand by Jesus no matter what (Matt. 26:33). He responds now with an over-my-dead-body reaction, brandishing his sword.[3]

> Simon Peter therefore having a sword, drew it, and struck the high priest's slave, and cut off his right ear;[4] and the slave's name was Malchus. (John 18:10)

A Remarkable Response

Jesus reproves His impulsive friend, asking him a question that raises an important issue.

> Jesus therefore said to Peter, "Put the sword into the sheath; the cup which the Father has given Me, shall I not drink it?" (v. 11)

---

3. Two types of swords were common in those days. One was large and heavy, designed to strike a fatal blow after being drawn over the head and brought down with full force. The other was more like a dagger, sharp on both edges, easily hidden, and able to be used swiftly. In all probability, the latter was the type Peter used that night.

4. Luke, the physician, makes note of Jesus healing the man's ear in Luke 22:51.

The words "the cup" take us back to Jesus' prayer in Gethsemane. He prayed that it would be taken from Him but still resigned Himself to the will of His Father. He was absolutely committed to fulfilling the Father's purpose for Him. Peter, on the other hand, was not. He lacked that important dimension of a disciple—an unreserved commitment to the Father's will, regardless of the personal consequences.

You and I . . . On Drinking the Cup God Gives Us

How does all this tie in to us, two thousand years later? For every disciple there is a purpose to be fulfilled, a mission, a mandate, a heaven-sent assignment. And with every purpose there is a cup to drink. It may range from a thorn in the flesh to nails that impale you to a cross. It may be an occasional hindrance or an ongoing obstacle. Whatever your cup, in it there is pain to be endured. There is affliction, heartache, disappointment. But through every pain there is a victory to be claimed.

The late George Matheson of Scotland echoes the significance of drinking the cup our Lord chooses for us.

> My soul, reject not the place of thy prostration! It has ever been thy robing-room for royalty. Ask the great ones of the past what has been the spot of their prosperity; they will say, "It was the cold ground on which I once was lying." Ask Abraham; he will point you to the sacrifice of Moriah. Ask Joseph; he will direct you to his dungeon. Ask Moses; he will date his fortune from his danger in the Nile. Ask Ruth; she will bid you build her monument in the field of her toil. Ask David; he will tell you that his songs came from the night. Ask Job; he will remind you that God answered him out of the whirlwind. . . . Ask Paul; he will attribute his inspiration to the light which struck him blind. Ask one more—the Son of Man. . . . He will answer, "From the cold ground on which I was lying—the Gethsemane ground; I received My sceptre there." . . . The cup thou fain wouldst pass from thee will be thy coronet in the sweet by-and-by. The hour of thy loneliness will crown thee. The day of thy depression will regale thee. It is thy *desert* that will break forth into singing; it is the trees of thy silent *forest* that will clap their hands.[5]

---

5. George Matheson, *Thoughts for Life's Journey* (New York, N.Y.: Hodder and Stoughton, n.d.), pp. 266–67.

◆

Our Father,

    We thank You for the serious words of Your Book and for the model of Christ, who perfectly lived out the truths we find there. Thank You for the wounds and scars that give us wisdom and character. Forgive us for short-circuiting pain and for taking shortcuts to maturity, for simulating submission rather than living it.

    Find in us acceptable wills and surrendered hearts. And as You give us the cup, enable us, our Father, to accept it . . . to drink it . . . and to let You bring victory through it, even though at the time it seems impossible. We love You, Father, with all our hearts. Amen.

 Living Insights

The problem of pain and suffering is not an abstract one; it touches each of us. At some time or other we all shoulder the yoke of suffering. Whether we bear up under the load or buckle is largely determined by the strength of our faith.

To strengthen yours, we recommend the following helpful books.

Affliction, by Edith Schaeffer

The Problem of Pain, by C. S. Lewis

Where Is God When It Hurts? by Philip Yancey

Edith Schaeffer's book draws upon a number of biblical texts as it takes a compassionate look at the reality of suffering in our lives. *The Problem of Pain* is more philosophical in nature. Philip Yancey's book won the Gold Medallion for the best inspirational book of 1977. All are excellent, but if you have time for just one, we suggest that you read *Where Is God When It Hurts?*

If you would like a list of books for specific areas of pain—from alcoholism to an unbelieving spouse—write to Insight for Living and request the pamphlet *Books for Those Who Hurt.* It was compiled by our Counseling Department and gives recommendations for books in forty categories of painful situations.

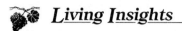 **_Living Insights_**

What is the cup God has presently placed before *you?*

_____

Are you in your own Gethsemane, wrestling with God, or have you resigned yourself to take whatever He sees fit to send your way?

_____

_____

What are your reservations about taking the cup?

_____

_____

_____

In what way would your refusal to take the cup alter your circumstances?

_____

_____

_____

How would your refusal affect your relationship with God?

_____

_____

Reflect on Lamentations 3:1–38. Describe the prophet's suffering.

_____

_____

_____

What changed his attitude from bitterness to thanksgiving?

_____

_____

Chapter 14

HOW LONG HAS THIS BEEN HAPPENING?

Mark 9:14–29

Fatherhood is no easy task, even for the best of men. Juggling the responsibilities of providing and parenting keeps just about every father in a constant state of guilt for not doing enough in either area.

One thing all fathers need is the respect of their children. Sometimes fathers forfeit that respect by irresponsible or abusive behavior. But sometimes that respect is eroded by the constant carping of a demeaning wife. Lewis Yablonsky writes candidly of his mother's habit of destroying the respect he might otherwise have had for his own dad.

> I vividly recall sitting at the dinner table with my two brothers and father and mother and cringing at my mother's attacks on my father. "Look at him," she would say . . . , "his head and shoulders are bent down. He's a failure. He doesn't have the courage to get a better job or make more money. He's a beaten man." He would keep his eyes pointed toward his plate and never answer her. She never extolled his virtue of persistence or the fact that he worked so hard; instead she constantly focused on the negative and created an image to his three sons of a man without fight, crushed by a world over which he had no control.
>
> His not fighting back against her constant criticism had the effect of confirming its validity to her sons. I have to add that my mother's treatment and depiction of my father did not convey to me that marriage was a happy state of being. . . . I was not especially motivated to assume the role of husband and father myself from my observations of my whipped father. . . .
>
> My overall research clearly supports the fact that the mother is a basic filter and has enormous significance in the father-son relationship.[1]

1. Lewis Yablonsky, *Fathers and Sons* (New York, N.Y.: Simon and Schuster, 1982), p. 134.

In today's lesson we want to reverse the trend of dumping on dads. We want to stand up and give three cheers for all the dads who care—and especially for one committed dad we'll read about in Mark 9:14–29.

Three Cheers for Fathers Who Care

Cheer number one is for fathers who consider their work important but their home essential. This all boils down to an issue of priorities. Even though work is high on the list, it should never supersede the priority of a healthy home life. It's important to remember that the investment with the greatest dividend is not in the stock market or in oil or real estate; it's in the people we love who live in our own homes.

Cheer number two is for fathers who love their wives but who have plenty of affection left over for their children. The best fathers are good husbands, husbands who love their wives in a warm and affectionate way. And it seems like those husbands are the ones who have enough love left over to spread around to all the children.

Cheer number three is for fathers who not only listen to and respect their children but who listen even better to and have even greater respect for God. Some men are reluctant to cultivate such a heart for God because they think it will emasculate them. Just the opposite is true. Instead of diminishing manliness, a close walk with God enhances it. Nothing exudes masculine strength more than a deep, unswerving relationship with God.

If you had a father who kept his priorities straight between work and home, if you had a father who was expressive with his love, if you had a father who respected you but respected God even more, then stand up proudly and give him three cheers, won't you?

A First-Century Struggle and Solution

In Mark 9:2–13, Jesus and three of His closest disciples share an incredible moment together on the Mount of Transfiguration. But as they wend their way down the sloping shoulders of the mountain, they find themselves enveloped by a large crowd and a babel of argumentative scribes.

> And when they came back to the [other] disciples, they saw a large crowd around them, and some scribes arguing with them. And immediately, when the entire crowd saw Him, they were amazed, and began running up to greet Him. And He asked them, "What are you discussing with them?" (vv. 14–16)

Discussion of the Problem

The debate between the disciples and the scribes centers around a boy inhabited by a demon. The nine disciples left on the foothills of the mountain are helpless to exorcise it. All the scribes can do is point fingers and criticize. Meanwhile, off to the side, a father stands wringing his hands. As Jesus enters the circle of debate, this father, who cares deeply for his victimized son, steps forward to present his case.

> And one of the crowd answered Him, "Teacher, I brought You my son, possessed with a spirit which makes him mute; and whenever it seizes him, it dashes him to the ground and he foams at the mouth, and grinds his teeth, and stiffens out. And I told Your disciples to cast it out, and they could not do it." (vv. 17–18)

With a physician's attention to detail, Luke gives an even more vivid description of the boy's symptoms: "a spirit seizes him, and he suddenly screams, and it throws him into a convulsion with foaming at the mouth, and as it mauls him, it scarcely leaves him" (9:39).

The challenge of parenting a child with seizures is one thing; add a demon to the equation and the challenge becomes a nightmare. Luke also mentions that the boy is the father's only son (v. 38). Possibly, he is even the only child. And when you add that frame to the tragic picture, it sets the scene off as being even more heartrending.

Mingled with Jesus' compassion for the father is a deep sense of frustration.

> And He answered them and said, "O unbelieving generation, how long shall I be with you? How long shall I put up with you? Bring him to Me!" (Mark 9:19)

In response to Jesus' words, the demon, like a recalcitrant child throwing a temper tantrum in a losing battle with a parent, hurls the boy to the ground in a last-ditch effort to assert authority.

> And they brought the boy to Him. And when he saw Him, immediately the spirit threw him into a convulsion, and falling to the ground, he began rolling about and foaming at the mouth. (v. 20)

Conversation with the Father

It's encouraging to see the father, as opposed to the mother, involved in this story. So often it's the mother who's left with the responsibility of caring for a sick child, but here we see the father taking an active role.

Jesus, the Great Physician, proceeds to get the boy's medical history.

> And He asked his father, "How long has this been happening to him?" And he said, "From childhood. And it has often thrown him both into the fire and into the water to destroy him. But if You can do any-thing, take pity on us and help us!" (vv. 21–22)

The father's painful description of his son's problems crescendoes into an impassioned plea. You can almost see the tears welling up in his eyes. You can almost hear his voice breaking. His words timidly reach out to Jesus, and the Savior bolsters the man's faith.

> And Jesus said to him, "'If You can!' All things are possible to him who believes." (v. 23)

What an incredible truth. There is no problem so severe that it lies beyond the reach of hands extended to heaven. As the man lifts his hands, honest emotions spill from his heart.

> Immediately the boy's father cried out and began say-ing, "I do believe; help my unbelief." (v. 24)

Relief from the Savior

> And when Jesus saw that a crowd was rapidly gather-ing, He rebuked the unclean spirit, saying to it, "You deaf and dumb spirit, I command you, come out of him and do not enter him again." And after crying out and throwing him into terrible convulsions, it came out; and the boy became so much like a corpse that most of them said, "He is dead!" But Jesus took him by the hand and raised him; and he got up. (vv. 25–27)

The word *unclean* comes from the Greek term *akathartos*. It is derived from the term *katharos*, meaning "clean, pure, free from anything that spoils, adulterates, or corrupts." The prefix reverses it to mean just the opposite. That is the evil nature of the spirit at work in the boy's life.

You can imagine the reaction of the father when his boy was purged of this unclean spirit. His years of pent-up tears must have flooded their banks. Finally, after all the painful past with this troubled boy, he receives his precious son back.

110

Reproof to the Disciples

Once out of the public eye, the disciples question Jesus about their inability to cast the demon out.

> And when He had come into the house, His disciples began questioning Him privately, "Why could we not cast it out?" And He said to them, "This kind cannot come out by anything but prayer." (vv. 28–29)

Jesus' answer is not complicated: *They were powerless because they were prayerless.* Where had they placed their trust? In themselves. Or perhaps in their past performance, for they had a pretty good track record at casting out demons (see Mark 6:7–13). But a past record of victories is no guarantee of continued ability to win and overcome. In prayer, we model total dependence on God, leaving no room for *our* power, *our* significance, or *our* glory.

Some Twentieth-Century Insights and Applications

In this dramatic passage we see a father emotionally involved with his son's life; we see disciples who are powerless; we see the Lord asking questions and making a difference.

As we step back from the biblical narrative, let's address a few questions that have an applicational edge for all of us today.

Have you neglected relationships in your home—has your job or other responsibilities kept you from being the involved parent you should be? Have you been living a spiritually depleted, prayerless life?

Or, like the father in the story, have you rolled up your sleeves to get directly involved with solving the problems that plague your children? Do you believe that "*all things* are possible to him who believes"?

Pretty hard questions to face. Think about them for a few minutes, and we'll give you an opportunity to answer them in the Living Insights that follow.

◆

Heavenly Father,

Thank You so much for our families. Thank You for the opportunities You give us to be involved in their lives, to influence their decisions, to bring them joy. We're sorry for the times we've taken those relationships for granted.

111

We ask Your forgiveness for our self-centeredness and for
our lack of participation in the concerns of their lives.

Help us, Father, to replenish the spiritual resources that
can help us meet their needs. Help us remember to spend
our time, our money, and our attention on those who are
dearest to our hearts. We pray in Your Son's name. Amen.

Living Insights

Have you neglected relationships in your home? _____

_____

If so, which relationship has suffered most? _____

_____

What could you do, starting today, to give that relationship the
attention it deserves?

1. _____

2. _____

3. _____

What one activity or responsibility could you drop to give yourself more time to devote to that relationship?

_____

What is the most painful problem that exists with any of your
children?

_____

_____

_____

What could you do to take a more active role in solving some
of the problems that plague your children?

_____

_____

_____

Do you believe that "*all things* are possible to him who believes"?

_____

_____

If so, then Jesus is the one you need to take that problem to. Won't you spend some time now praying for Him to intervene? And don't be ashamed if you have to pray as the father did in our passage: "I do believe; help my unbelief."

Living Insights

Have you been living a spiritually depleted life? _____

_____

What could you do to replenish those depleted resources?

_____

_____

Have you been leading a prayerless life? _____

_____

We often experience defeat in our prayer lives, not so much because of sin or sloth, but because of two simple procedural mistakes.

One, we don't schedule a regular time for prayer. Two, we don't know what to say.

The first can be solved by inking in a quiet time in your daily calendar—a time that's free from distractions and a time that won't get crowded off your schedule.

The second can be corrected by praying through Scripture, using the words found there as a springboard for your prayers. The Psalms are a good place to start.

For a little inspirational boost to get you started, pick up a copy of the classic InterVarsity Press booklet *My Heart—Christ's Home,* by Robert Boyd Munger.

Another book that might encourage you in this area is *Daring to Draw Near,* by John White. It is truly a thought-provoking and motivating book, also published by InterVarsity Press.

Chapter 15

DO YOU KNOW WHAT I HAVE DONE?

John 13:1–17

The New Testament is full of information about Jesus' life on earth—who He was, what He did, where He went, why He died. We're even allowed to eavesdrop on some of His conversations, to peer through time's windows and watch how He handled a variety of people and situations.

But only once in the entire New Testament do we hear from Jesus Himself about what He was like inside. Only once does He tell us in His own words about His personality, His temperament. We can read those words in Matthew 11:28–29.

> "Come to Me, all who are weary and heavy-laden, and
> I will give you rest. Take My yoke upon you, and learn
> from Me, for I am gentle and humble in heart; and
> you shall find rest for your souls."

There it is! Those verses contain an invitation, a promise, a couplet of commands . . . and a revealing self-description.

That self-description is also a rather surprising one. After all, He could have said, "I am powerful" or "I am all-wise." He could have told us, "I am in full control" or "I am holy, pure, undefiled." But He didn't. Of all the things He could have said with perfect truth, He chose to tell us, "I am gentle and humble in heart."

Those are interesting words in their original language. *Gentle* comes from the Greek term *praus*, which is used to describe a horse that has been broken and tamed. William Barclay defines it this way:

> There is gentleness in *praus* but behind the gentleness
> there is the strength of steel, for the supreme charac-
> teristic of the man who is *praus* is that he is the man
> who is under perfect control. It is not a spineless gen-
> tleness, a sentimental fondness, a passive quietism. It
> is a strength under control.[1]

1. William Barclay, *New Testament Words* (London, England: SCM Press, 1964), pp. 241–42.

The word *humble* is an altogether different term. It carries the idea of "stooping low," and it was used most often of a household servant—someone who would stoop over the cooking or the serving of meals or the washing of clothing. It has nothing to do with insignificance or weakness, but rather depicts someone who stoops low in order to serve another.

So Jesus, in that brief passage, gives us a picture of someone who restrains his or her own power, who deliberately chooses the role of a servant. Let's keep that picture in mind as we listen to one of the most searching and convicting questions Jesus asked while on earth. For what our Lord describes in Matthew 11, He demonstrates in John 13.

The Background: Matters of Historical Interest

Before we raise the curtain on the scene in John, let's get an overview of its historical context.

First, let's pinpoint the time. It is just before the Feast of the Passover, a time for reflecting upon the epochal event in ancient Jewish history when the Hebrews were delivered from Egyptian bondage. This was the most important feast on the Jewish calendar. Like our Thanksgiving dinner in some ways, it was a time for eating traditional dishes[2] and gathering with family and special friends.

Next, let's discuss who was present. At the start, there were thirteen—Jesus and all twelve of His disciples. By the end of the meal, there was one less. Judas, who was the betrayer, had been dismissed.

Last, let's examine the place. Its exact location is never named for us, but the other Gospel writers tell us it was an upper room somewhere in Jerusalem. It's an intimate setting, with close friends and flickering oil lamps, a setting we've often referred to as the Last Supper. It's the setting where Jesus will give His men their final marching orders . . . orders that will impact the world.

---

2. Our Thanksgiving meal usually contains traditional foods, but the dishes the Jews served at the Passover Feast had symbolic significance as well. Instead of corn and squash and beans, they served a strange mixture called *charoseth,* which represented the mortar with which their ancestors had made bricks while in bondage. Instead of turkey, they served lamb, the blood of which was shed so that the angel of death might pass over their houses. As such, it represented the Lamb of God yet to come. They also made bread without yeast to remind them of the haste in which they left Egypt and served bitter herbs that spoke of the bitterness of slavery. See *Celebrate the Feasts,* by Martha Zimmerman (Minneapolis, Minn.: Bethany House Publishers, 1981), pp. 64–66; and *The Zondervan Pictorial Encyclopedia* (Grand Rapids, Mich.: Zondervan Publishing House, Regency Reference Library, 1976), under "leaven."

But before those momentous last instructions can be given, Jesus has one final lesson to teach His disciples.

The Event: Example of Personal Humility

In the middle of this quiet meal, something strange occurs.

> Now before the Feast of the Passover, Jesus knowing that His hour had come that He should depart out of this world to the Father, having loved His own who were in the world, He loved them to the end. And during supper, the devil having already put into the heart of Judas Iscariot, the son of Simon, to betray Him, Jesus, knowing that the Father had given all things into His hands, and that He had come forth from God, and was going back to God, rose from supper, and laid aside His garments; and taking a towel, He girded Himself about. Then He poured water into the basin, and began to wash the disciples' feet, and to wipe them with the towel with which He was girded. (John 13:1–5)

Can you imagine a father halfway through his steak pushing back his chair, picking up a sponge, and beginning to wipe off the counters? The disciples must have been as surprised as you or I would be. Why on earth would Jesus do such a thing, especially during their last meal together?

There are two reasons, neither of which is stated by John and only one of which is mentioned by anyone in Scripture. We can infer the first reason from Luke 22:14–24, where we read that at this very meal the disciples have been arguing over which of them was the greatest. After three and a half years of following the Messiah, these men still haven't squelched the rivalry in their hearts. Jesus washes their feet to teach them a lesson about humility.

We can figure out the other reason by using common sense— their feet were dirty. Back then, the roads weren't paved. During the dry season, they were covered with a layer of dust, which became a layer of mud during the rainy season. Feet that traveled just stayed dirty; it was impossible to avoid. Even today, it is traditional in the Orient for shoes to be set aside at the door.

But in those days, tradition—and practicality—went a step further. For a formal gathering, the host would assign a servant to wait by the door with water and a towel. As the guests arrived, they would slip off their sandals and let the servant bathe their feet. For an informal gathering with friends or family, one member would volunteer to play the role of the servant.

But at this informal gathering, no one volunteered. The disciples were willing to fight over the throne, but not over the towel; they wanted to reign, not stoop. So Jesus, without a word, left His dinner and picked up a towel.

Sometimes the most effective rebuke is a silent one. The contrast between the heated words of the disciples and the cool splashing of water must have been striking. An embarrassed hush seems to have fallen over the room until Jesus reached the feet of Peter.

> And so He came to Simon Peter. He said to Him, "Lord, do You wash my feet?" Jesus answered and said to him, "What I do you do not realize now, but you shall understand hereafter." Peter said to Him, "Never shall You wash my feet!" (John 13:6–8a)

Here was pride exposed. You can almost see Peter tucking his feet under his robe, not wanting the dirt exposed, not wanting Christ to be the one to wash them. He had not yet learned that humility includes the rare ability to receive without embarrassment. Lest you think humility also means going along with everyone's wishes, that gentleness means being a doormat, take a look at Jesus' next words.

> Jesus answered him, "If I do not wash you, you have no part with Me." (v. 8b)

That's a pretty strong rebuke, coming from a servant! Peter gets the message and, true to form, overreacts.

> Simon Peter said to Him, "Lord, not my feet only, but also my hands and my head." (v. 9)

His motive is pure, but he's carried things too far. A full bath is not something to be done in public, but in private. It's a far more personal thing than just a foot rinse. Furthermore, spiritually speaking, once there has been an authentic expression of faith in Christ, an overall cleansing from sin is no longer needed. We just need a little wiping off now and then (1 John 1:9)—as they say in the South, a little spit bath just to get the dirty parts. And that's what Jesus points out to Peter.

> Jesus said to him, "He who has bathed needs only to wash his feet, but is completely clean; and you are clean, but not all of you." (v. 10)

Do you hear that pause after the second *clean?* You can feel the tension in the air as Jesus turns to the feet of Judas.

> For He knew the one who was betraying Him; for this
> reason He said, "Not all of you are clean." (v. 11)

True humility plays no favorites; it's neither selective nor exclusive. Even Judas, whose heart was filled with filthy plans, felt the touch of Jesus' hands as He rinsed away the outer dirt. There must have been a pin-drop silence in that Upper Room as Jesus laid aside the basin, folded the grimy towel, slipped back into His robe, and took His place at the table. And into that silence came the probing question that is the focus of our lesson today: "Do you know what I have done to you?" (v. 12b).

It's a question that is easy to overlook in a cursory reading of the passage. It's not one designed for an answer; it's a rhetorical question to make us think. What are the implications of what has just taken place? What is it supposed to tell us? Jesus' words go on.

> "You call Me Teacher and Lord; and you are right, for
> so I am. If I then, the Lord and the Teacher, washed
> your feet . . ." (vv. 13–14a)

Stop right there—don't even finish reading the verse. The obvious completion of the sentence would be, "then you should also wash Mine." Right? Turnabout's fair play—you scratch my back, I'll scratch yours. But that isn't how it goes.

> "If I then, the Lord and the Teacher, washed your feet,
> *you also ought to wash one another's feet.* For I gave you
> an example that you also should do as I did to you."
> (vv. 14–15, emphasis added)

Anyone would be glad to wash Jesus' feet. But somebody else's? Would you want to wash the feet of someone who would never wash yours in return? Or how about someone who is dirty . . . or smells?

But that's His message. And He gave it not just in words but in actions. He played the role of servant; He modeled what He wanted us to do. And had we been resting by that table in the flickering light of the Upper Room, it would have been an example we could never have forgotten.

The Promise: Assurance of Practical Importance

We could stop reading at verse 15. This part of the story's complete there; nothing more happens. But the next two verses give us principles to live by.

"Truly, truly, I say to you, a slave is not greater than his master; neither is one who is sent greater than the one who sent him. If you know these things, you are blessed if you do them." (vv. 16–17)

The first principle is this: *Humility is revealed by acknowledging the greatness of another* (v. 16). Have you ever been to the symphony? If you have, you may remember that the conductor, at the first sign of applause, turns to wave the credit on to the orchestra. That conductor is acknowledging that he or she would merely be waving a baton if it weren't for those who play violin or oboe or percussion. That's humility.

The second principle is *happiness results from demonstrating humility toward others* (v. 17). "Happy"—that's what the word *blessed* means. But happiness doesn't come from just understanding about humility. It doesn't come from merely sitting in on an Upper Room lesson. It's a result of humility as a way of life.

◆

Our Lord,

> We understand what it's like to be weary and heavy-laden; exhaustion is nothing new to us. But we confess that there is no exhaustion like the weariness of trying to work our way to glory, and there is no burden like the heavy-laden one that comes with a life of sin and failure and guilt and remorse. May we hear the splashing of water in our lives today. May we feel the warmth of the towel at our feet. And may we respond to the gentle wooing of Your Spirit. We come in our pride and in our sin, but we also come in the lovely name of Jesus Christ our Lord. Amen.

 Living Insights
STUDY ONE

At the beginning of our study we read the only words in Scripture that paint a self-portrait of Jesus' heart: "For I am gentle and humble in heart."

If you had only one opportunity and just a few words to describe yourself, what would you say?

_____

_____

Are the words you just wrote a description you feel satisfied with? Is it one that would be pleasing to the Lord?

_____

Jesus chose the words *gentle* and *humble* out of all the words He could have chosen. What do you think is the significance of that?

_____

_____

_____

Humility is often a hard quality to demonstrate, let alone truly feel. Why do you think this is?

_____

_____

_____

_____

Is there anyone in your life you have an especially hard time being humble around? What might you do to overcome that problem?

_____

_____

_____

Living Insights   STUDY TWO

We've been concentrating mainly on the self-description part of Matthew 11:28–29, but those two verses also contain an invitation, a promise, and two commands. Let's take a closer look at those other parts, starting with the invitation: "Come to Me, all who are weary and heavy-laden."

Can there be a more comforting verse anywhere in Scripture? What kind of look do you imagine was on Jesus' face as He spoke those words? How do you imagine He was standing?

_____

_____

Let's go on to the promise: "I will give you rest." Are you in need of rest today? What are the burdens that are wearing you out?

_____

_____

_____

What does Jesus mean by His two commands: "Take My yoke upon you, and learn from Me"? How do you think following them might bring rest for your soul?

_____

_____

_____

Before closing the book on this study, won't you take Jesus up on His invitation and lay your burdens at His feet? Take some time now to pour your heart out to Him. Ask for His help in following His commands. And may the consolation of His love envelop you.

Chapter 16

SHALL NOT GOD BRING ABOUT JUSTICE?

Luke 18:1–8

On November 27, 1976, a drifter named Randall Dale Adams made a mistake. It was a mistake that cost him twelve and a half years in a Texas prison, and almost cost him his life.

On that day, Adams hitched a ride with 16-year-old David Ray Harris. On November 28, at about 12:30 A.M., one of them allegedly shot police officer Robert Wood five times at point-blank range, leaving him to die in the freezing cold Dallas midnight.

Here are the facts of the case:

David Ray Harris was a known felon. He was driving a stolen car and carrying a stolen gun. He had dropped Adams off at a motel at 10 P.M. on the twenty-seventh, and the next day bragged to friends about "offing a pig" the night before.

But David Ray Harris testified that Adams was the one who pulled the trigger. As a result of that testimony, Adams was given the death sentence, which was later commuted to life in prison.

If it weren't for a film-maker-turned-private-eye, Randall Adams would still be in jail today. But when Errol Morris accidentally stumbled across Adams' story, he thought something seemed wrong. After two years of investigation and the making of a movie called *The Thin Blue Line*, a hearing revealed the distortion of evidence at Adams' original trial, and Adams was finally freed.

This story had a happy ending; justice *was* eventually served. But it isn't always, is it? You and I could rattle off a dozen examples of unfair treatment . . . an immoral businessperson getting away scot-free with unethical dealings; a criminal being released because of some loophole in the law; an innocent child being abused. And if we allow ourselves to think much about it, questions can't help but arise in our minds. Questions like, Where is God in all this? What can I do about it? How can I best respond?

For the sake of this study, we'll define *justice* as right being rewarded and wrong being punished, regardless of race, age, sex, nationality, or economic status. We'll attempt to answer our agonizing questions with insight from Luke 18 . . . but be forewarned: the answer is one you may not be ready to accept.

A Parable That Gives Us Hope

The passage we're going to study may not give us the answer we want to hear, but its simple words will give us a ray of hope. Before we start, however, let's nail down the meaning of the word *parable*, since that's the term used to introduce the story Jesus tells.

The dictionary says that a parable is a "short fictitious story that illustrates a moral attitude or a religious principle."[1] The term itself is Greek: *para*, meaning "to place something alongside something else"; and *bole*, from the word *ballō*, meaning "to throw." So a parable is a story in which the teller uses an understood truth about everyday life to teach something that is unknown, placing the familiar along-side the unfamiliar to illustrate one major truth.

Most of the parables in the Bible don't have a stated purpose, but the one in Luke 18 is an exception.

> Now He was telling them a parable to show that
> at all times they ought to pray and not to lose heart.
> (v. 1)

Lose heart . . . isn't that exactly what we tend to do when we come across injustice? Jesus is telling us from the start that prevailing prayer will be our greatest ammunition when we're fighting with the enemy of discouragement.

Now that we have a feel for its purpose, let's go on to analyze the story.

> "There was in a certain city a judge who did not fear
> God, and did not respect man. And there was a widow
> in that city, and she kept coming to him, saying, 'Give
> me legal protection from my opponent.' And for a
> while he was unwilling; but afterward he said to him-
> self, 'Even though I do not fear God nor respect man,
> yet because this widow bothers me, I will give her legal
> protection, lest by continually coming she wear me
> out.'" (vv. 2–5)

In this simple story there are just two characters. It will help us see the contrasts between them if we list their qualities in columns.

---

1. *Webster's Ninth New Collegiate Dictionary*, see "parable."

The Woman	The Man
• Helpless; a widow	• Powerful; a judge
• Courageous	• Lacks integrity
• Needs justice—protection from opponent	• Has power to provide protection
• Persistent in her request	• Has to put up with her persistence
• At the judge's mercy	• Finally grants her request

Here we have a widow who is being harassed to the point of needing legal protection, and a judge who not only has no respect for God but none for people either. At the outset, it doesn't appear likely that she's going to get any help. But the judge finally gives in, "lest . . . she wear me out." There's humor in that phrase; it literally means "hit me under the eye." The judge can see that this woman means business, and sheer weariness of her daily presence makes him give in to her request.

And there the story ends . . . but not the Lord's teaching. In verses 6–8, things start to get personal.

> And the Lord said, "Hear what the unrighteous judge said; now shall not God bring about justice for His elect, who cry to Him day and night, and will He delay long over them? I tell you that He will bring about justice for them speedily. However, when the Son of Man comes, will He find faith on the earth?"

Almost all of us know what it's like to live in an unbearable situation without the power or skill to get ourselves out. And many of us know how it feels when the person we turn to for assistance seems to have little concern either for justice in general or for us in particular. But here, surprisingly, Jesus changes the focus from an unjust human judge to the one holy and righteous judge, the almighty God. He's setting up yet another contrast. If a judge like the one in the story will eventually give in to what's right, can't we count on our loving Lord, who is perfectly just and good, to provide justice as well?

Of course we can. But there's a comparison in this story as well as a contrast. The link is *persistence,* the constant coming, the day-and-night petitioning. Sound impossible to carry out? Read what G. Campbell Morgan said about prayer.

Prayer is far more than uttering words. I can pray when I do not think I am praying. We can pray without any words at all. Prayer, in the last analysis, is the urge of the life towards God, and spiritual things; the setting of the mind upon things above, as Paul has it. Every detail of every day can be mastered by that urge.[2]

It doesn't take a seminary degree to pray effectively. It doesn't take a day without interruptions, nor special words or special postures. It just takes a heart that yearns for right, a heart demanding that justice be served. It takes crying out, "Help, Lord! Make it right!" when there's nothing else to be done.

The crucial question for our study is this: "Shall not God bring about justice?" In answer, we have a promise straight from the lips of Jesus: "Our God will not only administer justice, He will do so speedily!"

But that's where our faith flags. How can we believe in God's justice, when we know people right this minute who are experiencing outrageous injustice, and nothing is being done to stop it?

This is where we have to stop and consider the context of this promise. In chapter 18, verse 1, there's a little word which clues us in that we need to take a look backward: "Now He was telling *them* a parable" (emphasis added). Who is "them"? To find out, we have to retrace our steps to verse 22 of chapter 17—the "them" is the disciples, since no other group is mentioned between 17:22 and 18:1. And in the context of chapter 17, Jesus is talking about the last days, when He will return to earth. He's talking about the time when the Judge will come back, when wrong will be made right, when righteousness will rule and the unrighteous will pay.

And it is *in those last days* that justice will take place speedily.[3] At that point in time, every wrong ever done will be righted.

There's another question tucked in at the end of the parable in Luke 18. It's a question not for the end times, but for the meantime. "Will He find faith on the earth?"

At first glance, that question may seem irrelevant. We've been talking about injustice, not faith. Yet faith is often the first thing

2. G. Campbell Morgan, *The Gospel According to Luke* (New York, N.Y.: Fleming H. Revell Co., n.d.), pp. 202–3.

3. For other references to the speed at which things will change when the Lord returns, see 1 Corinthians 15:51–52; 1 Thessalonians 4:17; and Revelation 6:14, 20:11, 21:1–4.

to go when injustice seems to prevail. In faith's place, bitterness and vengeance can creep in and consume, bringing the dark night of depression instead of the bright hope of prayer. Elie Wiesel, a Jewish survivor of the Nazi concentration camps, is an example of one who lost his hope. Read of the desolation that a dearth of faith brings.

> Never shall I forget that night, the first night in camp, which has turned my life into one long night, seven times cursed and seven times sealed. Never shall I forget that smoke. Never shall I forget the little faces of the children, whose bodies I saw turned into wreaths of smoke beneath a silent blue sky.
>
> Never shall I forget those flames which consumed my faith forever.
>
> Never shall I forget that nocturnal silence which deprived me, for all eternity, of the desire to live. Never shall I forget those moments which murdered my God and my soul and turned my dreams to dust. Never shall I forget these things, even if I am condemned to live as long as God Himself. Never.[4]

We can't deny Wiesel the horror of what he experienced any more than we can give back to Randall Dale Adams the years he spent in prison. Yet to both of those men we can say, "The story isn't over. There is a righteous God. Justice will be done."

A Concluding Word

If you are suffering an injustice right now, the night may seem long, the darkness complete. Perhaps you have given up hoping to see the light of God's justice.

But maybe it will help to know when you can expect justice to come . . . for you *can* expect it. And maybe it will help to know that God has given us a candle to light up our meantime—prayer. Not the pious words of a supersaint, but, as Paul describes, "groanings too deep for words" (Rom. 8:26). For those deep-felt prayers light up the darkness enough to remind us that God is there—enough to show us where to reach for His comforting hand.

---

4. Elie Wiesel, *Night*, trans. Stella Rodway (New York, N.Y.: Hill and Wang, 1960; New York, N.Y.: Bantam Books, 1982), p. 32.

Righteous Father,

Forgive us for the hours we've spent dwelling on wrongs done rather than praying for justice. Forgive us for the vengeful thoughts we have toward our enemies, toward those who have taken advantage of us. Refocus us, Father, as we see the power of prevailing prayer. Take away the bitterness, that acid which eats away at our souls and robs us of our hope. Turn us back to the Cross that we might see victory beyond the grave and hope beyond the loss. And keep us in faith, our Father, even when we are surrounded by injustice. We pray for Jesus' sake and in His name alone. Amen.

 ## Living Insights

In our study, we took a good look at the contrast between the woman and the judge in Jesus' parable. But we didn't take time to compare in detail that unrighteous judge and our own just Judge, our heavenly Father. Let's do that now.

Fill in the following chart with your own observations. What words would you use to describe the judge in the story? Now think of God in His role of judge. What words come to mind to describe Him?

The Unrighteous Judge	God as Judge

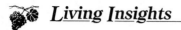 *Living Insights*

"Shall not God bring about justice?" "Will He find faith on the earth?" We need to take both of those questions out of the theoretical realm and into our daily lives.

Has your understanding of the timing of God's justice changed as a result of our study today? Summarize what you think Christ meant by His promise to bring about justice.

_____

_____

_____

_____

_____

If justice is promised as a future event, rather than one we can count on happening right now, can the hope of it bring us any comfort? Explain your answer.

_____

_____

_____

_____

_____

When Christ comes back, will He find any faith in your heart? We tend to feel the same way about that question as we felt about this one when we were kids: "When Mom gets home, will your room be cleaned up?" It seems to hold out more of a threat than it does hope! Yet faith is not meant to be a dreaded chore; it's intended to be a joy, something to cling to when things get tough. We ought to view that question more like we'd view this one: "When Mom gets home, will she find you enjoying the chocolate chip cookies she left for your snack?"

If Christ were to return today, what degree of faith would He find in your heart? Use the scale below, with 10 representing unwavering faith.

1   2   3   4   5   6   7   8   9   10

If your faith were just a little bit stronger, what new qualities might you find in your life? How might they help you when you're faced with injustice?

_____

_____

_____

_____

_____

_____

Before you turn the page, spend a final few moments praying about the unjust situations you are confronted with right now. They may be ones you are personally involved in, or they may be ones you know about secondhand. Either way, bring them before the Lord, the way the widow in the story brought her requests before the judge.

Chapter 17

WHY DO YOU STAND LOOKING INTO THE SKY?

Acts 1:1–11

A revolutionary lives in Cavendish, Vermont. Not the kind who carries guns or trains guerrillas. This man leads his revolution with his pen.

He doesn't fit the stereotype of a revolutionary. He isn't a youthful firebrand, full of stormy rhetoric and radical ideas. He's a soft-spoken seventy-year-old, a quiet intellectual with a wife and four sons. And instead of rallying crowds around him, he shuns public attention.

He lives on a fifty-acre estate where he sequesters himself away to fight his battle against communism, one sentence at a time. There he drones away at his task, twelve hours a day, seven days a week—studying, writing, typesetting, proofreading.

His name? Aleksandr Solzhenitsyn.

One cannot study Solzhenitsyn's life without being reminded of another revolutionary—Jesus Christ. He didn't fit that mold either. But what a revolution He led. Today we want to examine His revolution by looking at the first eleven verses of the book of Acts, a book which could well be subtitled "The Story of a Revolution."

The Ending That Started a Revolution

Acts was essentially written as a sequel to Luke's Gospel. The physician wrote the Acts of the Apostles for a high official in the Roman government, who most likely was seeking reliable evidence upon which to base his faith.

> The first account I composed, Theophilus, about all that Jesus began to do and teach, until the day when He was taken up. (Acts 1:1–2a)

Jesus' Ascension abruptly closes the final chapter of Luke's Gospel, but it opens the first chapter not only in the book of Acts but also in the history of the Christian revolution. Why would we say that? Well, during His earthly life and ministry, Jesus selected a group of men into whom He poured His life. But they never really got the message "until the day when He was taken up." That's when they were galvanized into action to carry on in His absence.

What empowered them to act was the coming of the Holy Spirit, who had played an integral part in commissioning them.

> After He had by the Holy Spirit given orders to the apostles whom He had chosen. (v. 2b)

That's what Luke hopes to impress upon Theophilus—that the revolution which burned in the hearts of the eleven was sparked from a divine fire. Jesus' method of revolution wasn't in passionate orations or indicting diatribes against the Roman government. It wasn't based on changing the economy or the environment or the social institutions. It was based on changing the human heart by the power of the Holy Spirit.

The Beginning That Required a Transition

What lit the fuse of the revolution in the hearts of the disciples was the resurrection of their leader from the dead.

> To these He also presented Himself alive, after His suffering, by many convincing proofs, appearing to them over a period of forty days, and speaking of the things concerning the kingdom of God. (v. 3)

For forty days Jesus not only convincingly demonstrated that He was alive, but He also took time to concentrate on teaching about the kingdom of God. It took awhile for it to soak into the disciples' minds that the kingdom Jesus was speaking of was not a political one but a spiritual one.

Earlier in the Upper Room, when Christ was preparing the disciples for His departure, He told them that He would not leave them as orphans. He promised to send the Holy Spirit to empower, enlighten, and encourage them in His absence.

> "And I will ask the Father, and He will give you another Helper, that He may be with you forever." (John 14:16)

> "The Helper, the Holy Spirit, whom the Father will send in My name, He will teach you all things, and bring to your remembrance all that I said to you." (v. 26)

> "When the Helper comes, whom I will send to you from the Father, that is the Spirit of truth, who proceeds from the Father, He will bear witness of Me." (15:26)

But between the time in the Upper Room and the time when the Holy Spirit was given, the disciples were forced to wait. They were to stay in Jerusalem and wait for Jesus to fulfill His promise (Acts 1:4).

Parenthetically, waiting is probably the most difficult part of the Christian life. God greatly rewards those who are willing to allow Him to work in His own time and in His own way (Isa. 40:31), but waiting is never easy, as this poem by Ruth Harms Calkin illustrates.

> Lord, I know there are countless times
> When I must wait patiently for You.
> Waiting develops endurance.
> It strengthens my faith
> And deepens my dependence upon You.
> I know You are Sovereign God—
> Not an errand boy
> Responding to the snap of my finger.
> I know Your timing is neatly wrapped
> In Your incomparable wisdom.
> But, Lord
> You have appointed prayer
> To obtain answers!
> Even David the Psalmist cried
> With confident boldness:
> "It is time, O Lord, for you to act."
> God, on this silent sunless morning
> When I am hedged in on every side
> I too cry boldly.
> You are my Father, and I am Your child.
> So, Lord, could You hurry a little?[1]

Certainly this is how the disciples felt as they were huddled together in Jerusalem, waiting for Jesus to fulfill His promise so that the revolution could begin.

Normally in a revolution, the tactics are obvious—demonstrations, the flexing of political muscle, intimidation, and threats. But none of these tactics are found in Jesus' revolution. Notice in Acts 1:5–8 how unique the dynamics of His revolution are. There are four of them; each forms a contrast with what you'd expect from an earthly revolution.

---

1. Ruth Harms Calkin, "Could You Hurry a Little," in *Lord, Could You Hurry a Little?* (Wheaton, Ill.: Tyndale House Publishers, Living Books, 1983), p. 37. Used by permission.

Jesus' Revolution Was Not Symbolic but a Reality

"For John baptized with water, but you shall be baptized
with the Holy Spirit not many days from now." (v. 5)

John offered water, but that only symbolized what was to come—
the actual presence of the Holy Spirit. He would invade their lives
and ignite their passions so that they would take the torch of revolution and spread the flame around the world.

Jesus' Revolution Was Based Not on a Program but on a Power

And so when they had come together, they were
asking Him, saying, "Lord, is it at this time You are
restoring the kingdom to Israel?" He said to them, "It
is not for you to know times or epochs which the
Father has fixed by His own authority; but you shall
receive power when the Holy Spirit has come upon
you." (vv. 6–8a)

The myopic disciples had their noses pressed to the calendar,
trying to discern a timetable for the coming of this kingdom that
Jesus had been preaching about so emphatically the past forty days.

But it wasn't important that they know God's timetable. What
was important was that they receive power from the Holy Spirit.
This same power that resurrected our Lord is the power that was to
come upon them. It is not the kind that breaks the sound barrier
or destroys whole towns. But no obstacle can withstand it, not even
the gates of hell. The word for this power is *dunamis*—the same
term from which we get the word *dynamite.*

Jesus' Revolution Depended Not on Promoters but on Witnesses

"And you shall be My witnesses." (v. 8b)

Jesus' revolutionary plan did not call for propagandists or politicians or promoters. It called for witnesses, those who could simply
share what they had seen and heard. This explains why Jesus spent
an additional forty days with the disciples, giving "convincing
proofs" and teaching them about the kingdom.

Jesus' Revolution Was not Limited but Universal

"Both in Jerusalem, and in all Judea and Samaria, and
even to the remotest part of the earth." (v. 8c)

No one was to be excluded from this revolutionary message.
Word was to go out to Jews and Gentiles, to slave and free, to
civilized countries and to the uttermost parts of the earth, no matter

how remote or barbaric. Christ's mission is for the world. It is not a treasure to be hoarded but a vision to be shared.

The Leaving That Prompted a Question

Of all the doctrines in Scripture having to do with Christ, perhaps the least mentioned is His triumphal reentry into heaven, referred to as the Ascension. Of all the Gospel writers, only Luke mentions it (Luke 24:51). Now, in his sequel, Luke describes the scene with a little more detail.

> And after He had said these things, He was lifted up while they were looking on, and a cloud received Him out of their sight. And as they were gazing intently into the sky while He was departing, behold, two men in white clothing stood beside them. (Acts 1:9–10)

The disciples stood looking into the air, awestruck, mouths hanging open, speechless. The silence was broken by two angels who were standing by.

> And they also said, "Men of Galilee, why do you stand looking into the sky? This Jesus, who has been taken up from you into heaven, will come in just the same way as you have watched Him go into heaven." (v. 11)

The crucial question was, "Why do you stand looking into the sky?" That's all it took to overcome the disciples' inertia and get them going. Luke 24:52 says that "they returned to Jerusalem with great joy." And there they stayed, waiting for the promise of the Holy Spirit to be fulfilled. Once it was, ten days later, the disciples were never the same.

The Question That Demands a Response

Ever since that day, the same question has needed to be asked—"Why stand there gazing into the sky?" Let's not spend our time staring off into space or quibbling over the prophetic timetable. Let's spend our time telling the world about our risen Savior.

That's exactly what those eleven men did who had been staring into the sky. As you trace their journeys through the travelogue of Acts, you'll see that they were obedient to the mandate of Acts 1:8.

They started in Jerusalem, then went out to Judea and Samaria, and finally, by the end of Acts, we find Paul picking up the torch passed to him and spreading the flame of the revolution to the natives in Malta (28:1–10). From there he set sail to Rome and boldly proclaimed the revolutionary message that shook the pillars of the Roman Empire (28:16–31).

Two thousand years ago a torch was lit to fuel a worldwide revolution. From generation to generation that torch has passed to faithful hands who have carried that light to the uttermost parts of the earth.

How firmly have you held that torch in your own home? How high have you held it in your own community? How faithfully have you passed it on to those who would follow after you?

If the revolution is to spread, *we* must be the ones to touch others with its flame. That's the only way the light of the gospel will be seen, and the only way the darkness will be dispelled.

* * *

Our Father,

Thank You for the passion and zeal and determination that only the presence of Your Spirit can bring. Forgive our months and even years of staring into the sky, of waiting for Your return without heeding Your final request. Lift us above our own petty and, in many ways, insignificant desires. And remind us of a world that has lost its way, of the people who have no idea of how to find their way home. Help us remember that You want to reach that world through us as we recommit ourselves to that eternal task. In the name of Jesus Christ our Lord and revolutionary Savior, we pray. Amen.

 Living Insights STUDY ONE

Acts 1:8 records the last words Jesus spoke while He was on earth. Undoubtedly they were some of His most important.

"But you shall receive power when the Holy Spirit has come upon you; and you shall be My witnesses both in Jerusalem, and in all Judea and Samaria, and even to the remotest part of the earth."

Let's dissect this crucial verse and scrutinize every part by answering the following questions.

135

1. What contrast is set up by the word "but"?

_____

_____

_____

2. What is the significance of the tense of the verb "shall receive"?

_____

_____

_____

3. What are the ramifications of the verb "receive"?

_____

_____

_____

4. How would power manifest itself in the witness of the disciples?

Acts 3:1–10 _____

_____

Acts 4:31–33 _____

_____

Acts 5:12 _____

_____

5. What is the significance of the dependent clause "when the Holy Spirit has come upon you"?

_____

_____

_____

6. Define *witness*.

_____

_____

7. How does the possessive pronoun "My" add to your understanding of the role of a witness?

_____

_____

8. Get a Bible atlas, or use the map in the back of your Bible, and locate the geographical points mentioned in verse 8. What pattern do you see emerging?

_____

_____

9. What principle can you derive from that pattern?

_____

_____

_____

10. Read Acts 2:1–4:33 to see how the promise of Acts 1:8 was fulfilled.

11. What personal application can you derive from your study of Acts 1:8?

_____

_____

_____

_____

Living Insights

Central to Acts 1:8 is the mandate to be witnesses. Everyone has an idea of what it means to be a witness for Christ, from passing out gospel tracts in a shopping mall to bringing the unsaved to an evangelistic rally.

The following couple of quotes about witnessing are worth not only meditating on but memorizing. Write them on an index card and go over them several times until they begin to permeate your thinking.

We do not draw people to Christ by loudly discrediting what they believe, by telling them how wrong they are and how right we are, but by showing them a light that is so lovely that they want with all their hearts to know the source of it.[2]

To be a witness does not consist in engaging in propaganda, nor even in stirring people up, but in being a living mystery. It means to live in such a way that one's life would not make sense if God did not exist.[3]

2. Madeleine L'Engle, *Walking on Water: Reflections on Faith and Art* (Wheaton, Ill.: Harold Shaw Publishers, 1980), p. 122.

3. Emmanuel, Cardinal Suhard, as quoted by L'Engle in *Walking on Water*, p. 31.

Chapter 18

SHARING THE
MEANING OF LIFE

Matthew 26:36–50, 28:1–8

Questions—that's what this series has been all about. Questions that raise key issues about life. We want to conclude by asking a few more questions: Have you ever been hailed one day, only to be nailed the next? Ever spent a sleepless night struggling with God's will? Ever felt so alone you could just die?

Those three questions can best be answered by a fourth: *Who hasn't?* At some time or another we've all felt rejected, uncertain, and alone.

But no one has felt more rejected, more uncertain, more alone than Jesus did the night of His betrayal. Let's cup our ears to hear His cries in that lonely garden on the Mount of Olives.

> Look closely through the shadowy foliage. See that person? See that solitary figure? What's he doing? Flat on the ground. Face stained with dirt and tears. Fists pounding the hard earth. Eyes wide with a stupor of fear. Hair matted with salty sweat. Is that blood on his forehead?
> That's Jesus. Jesus in the Garden of Gethsemane.
> . . .
> Does this look like the picture of a saintly Jesus resting in the palm of God? Hardly. . . . We see an agonizing, straining, and struggling Jesus. We see a "man of sorrows." We see a man struggling with fear, wrestling with commitments, and yearning for relief.[1]

In today's lesson we want to peer further into that garden. There we will see Jesus begging. There we will see Him betrayed. And there we will see a High Priest who can identify with our rejection, our uncertainty, and our loneliness.

This message was not a part of the original series but is compatible with it.

1. Max Lucado, *No Wonder They Call Him the Savior* (Portland, Oreg.: Multnomah Press, 1986), pp. 131–32.

139

Jesus Begs the Father

In Matthew 26:36–42, the writer sketches the scene with a charcoal pencil that shades the deity of our Savior with the dark, muted overtones of His humanity.

> Then Jesus came with them to a place called Gethsemane, and said to His disciples, "Sit here while I go over there and pray." And He took with Him Peter and the two sons of Zebedee, and began to be grieved and distressed. Then He said to them, "My soul is deeply grieved, to the point of death; remain here and keep watch with Me." And He went a little beyond them, and fell on His face and prayed, saying, "My Father, if it is possible, let this cup pass from Me; yet not as I will, but as Thou wilt." And He came to the disciples and found them sleeping, and said to Peter, "So, you men could not keep watch with Me for one hour? Keep watching and praying, that you may not enter into temptation; the spirit is willing, but the flesh is weak." He went away again a second time and prayed, saying, "My Father, if this cannot pass away unless I drink it, Thy will be done."

The text says He was "grieved and distressed," so much so that He teetered on the brink of death (vv. 37, 38). Why? Because He knew that, in spite of His being hailed only days before (21:9), He would be nailed in a few short hours. Because He had spent a sleepless night struggling with God's will. And because He felt so alone He could just die.

Jesus emerged from the winepress of that ordeal a crushed man. But out of that crushing experience came the most significant decision ever made—the decision to surrender to God.

Jesus Is Betrayed by a Friend

The scene grows ever darker, first from the lethargy of His closest confidants, then from the treachery of His betrayer.

> And again He came and found them sleeping, for their eyes were heavy. And He left them again, and went away and prayed a third time, saying the same thing once more. Then He came to the disciples, and said to them, "Are you still sleeping and taking your rest? Behold, the hour is at hand and the Son of Man is being betrayed into the hands of sinners. Arise, let us

be going; behold, the one who betrays Me is at hand!"

And while He was still speaking, behold, Judas, one of the twelve, came up, accompanied by a great multitude with swords and clubs, from the chief priests and elders of the people. Now he who was betraying Him gave them a sign, saying, "Whomever I shall kiss, He is the one; seize Him." And immediately he went to Jesus and said, "Hail, Rabbi!" and kissed Him. (26:43–49)

There is nothing more devastating than being betrayed by a friend. Perhaps something like that has happened to you; someone with whom you've had a close relationship has turned on you. A spouse. A boss. A roommate. A relative. A business partner. Some Judas, disguised as a friend, who betrayed you with a deceitful kiss (see Prov. 27:6).

As we return to our scene in Gethsemane, the night grows darker. The soldiers seize Jesus (Matt. 26:50). Then all the disciples flee (v. 56). Finally, those who have seized Him lead Him away (v. 57).

The tragic story that ensues is painful to read, despite its familiarity. Michael Green summarizes the gruesome events.

He was a travelling teacher, a jobbing builder by trade, and he had fallen foul of the authorities. After a burlesque of a trial he was led out to die outside the city walls of Jerusalem, the main town of one of the most insignificant provinces on the edge of the Roman map. The year was about A.D. 30. The date, Easter. The time, nine o'clock in the morning. They crucified him. Not at all pleasant, but it happened to a great many people in those days. No worse than what takes place in the torture chambers of more than seventy countries in the modern world. And yet it has become the most famous death in history.

It was a messy business. . . .

The physical effects of crucifixion were appalling. Of all deaths it is the most lingering and agonising. The unnatural position of the body made every movement a pain. The suspension of the whole body on jagged iron nails (one dating from A.D. 50 has recently been discovered in Jerusalem) driven through the most sensitive nerve centres of the wrists and ankles, ensured constant exquisite torture. The wounds of the nails and the weals from the lash soon became inflamed and even gangrenous. The body's position hindered circulation and caused indescribable pain in the chest. A raging thirst set in, brought on by the burning sun. The flies were thick around the victim. The agony of crucifixion was terrible beyond words.[2]

Jesus Bridges the Gap

Seeing the horrors of the Cross, we're tempted to think twice about surrendering to God. But if we look beyond the brow of that cruel hill and angle our eyes upward to heaven, we see not agony but ecstasy. We see the climax to the unfolding drama of redemption. We see a righteous Judge satisfied with the payment for the debt incurred by sin (see Isa. 53:11). The debt had created an enormous chasm between humanity and Deity. The Cross, as grotesque as it was, bridged that gap.

Paul articulates the theology of the Cross in Romans 5:19, 21.

For as through the one man's disobedience the many were made sinners, even so through the obedience of the One the many will be made righteous. . . . As sin reigned in death, even so grace might reign through righteousness to eternal life through Jesus Christ our Lord.

The apostle expresses that theological truth more succinctly in 2 Corinthians 5:21.

[God] made Him who knew no sin to be sin on our behalf, that we might become the righteousness of God in Him.

Jesus Comes Back from the Grave

Had Jesus simply died, He would have gone down in history as nothing more than a martyr. But His Resurrection set Him apart from every prophet, priest, or religious teacher who ever lived. Just when things got darkest for those who loved Jesus, a ray of light pierced through the morning sky to give a dawn to their hope.

And the angel answered and said to the women, "Do not be afraid; for I know that you are looking for Jesus who has been crucified. He is not here, for He has

2. Michael Green, *The Empty Cross of Jesus*, The Jesus Library series (Downers Grove, Ill.: InterVarsity Press, 1984), pp. 21, 23.

risen, just as He said. Come, see the place where He was lying. And go quickly and tell His disciples that He has risen from the dead; and behold, He is going before you into Galilee, there you will see Him; behold, I have told you." And they departed quickly from the tomb with fear and great joy and ran to report it to His disciples. (Matt. 28:5–8)

Let's go back to the three questions we asked at the beginning of our lesson. Ever been hailed one day and crucified the next? Ever spent a sleepless night struggling with God's will? Ever felt so alone you could just die?

If so, you need a ray of resurrection hope to shine on your life. But just as the dawn never comes without the night, so resurrection never comes without death.

Won't you surrender to the will of the Father? Maybe you've been wrestling in a Gethsemane of your own and are grieved and distressed to the point of death. Maybe it's time to stop resisting the cup the Father has set before you. Maybe it's time to surrender and say, "Lord, not *my* will be done but *Yours.*"

Jesus Has Paid for Our Release

Years ago, Dr. A. J. Gordon gave an illustration from the pulpit of his Boston church that explained the Cross better than any text of theology ever could.

One Sunday morning, the people came in and the choir met as usual. But sitting beside the pulpit was an old, beat-up, rusty birdcage. Dr. Gordon came to the pulpit and held up the empty cage. Then he told them this story.

It seems that one day he met a little boy in front of the church. He was carrying a rusty old birdcage in his hands, with several little birds clinging to the bottom of the cage. Dr. Gordon stopped him and asked,

> "Son, where did you get those birds?" The boy answered, "I trapped them out in the field." "What are you going to do with them?" the preacher asked. "I'm going to take them home and play with them and have some fun with them." "What will you do with them when you get through playing with them?" Dr. Gordon asked. "Oh," said the boy, "I guess I'll just feed them to an old cat we have around the house."

143

Then Dr. Gordon asked the boy how much he would take for the birds and the boy answered, "Mister, you don't want these birds. They're just little old field birds and they can't sing very well." Dr. Gordon said, "I'll give you two dollars for the cage and the birds." "All right," said the boy, "It's a deal, but you're making a bad bargain."

The exchange was made and the boy went whistling down the street, happy because he had two dollars in his pocket. Dr. Gordon took the cage out behind his church and opened the door of the cage and the birds flew out and went soaring away into the blue, singing as they went.

. . . [Dr. Gordon told his congregation,] "That little boy said that the birds could not sing very well, but when I released them from the cage they went singing away into the blue, and it seems that they were singing, 'Redeemed, redeemed, redeemed.' "[3]

Jesus Christ paid His tears and His blood and His life when He bought us from Satan's hand. And when He walked away a few hours later, He lifted the door to our cage and set us free. That's why His Resurrection is so important. Without it, life doesn't have any meaning, and we're not free. We're just trapped in a cage, lost and hopeless.

We can't promise that if you surrender to Christ, all your problems will be solved. In fact, surrender could lead to death—the death of a dream, the death of a career, the death of a relationship, the death of your old way of life. But we can guarantee that if you surrender to the will of the Father, you will have the hope of resurrection—physically, spiritually, and in every area of your life.

---◆---

Our Father,

Thank You for Christ, who has loved us and given Himself for us. Thank You for the eternal bridge that He built at the place of disaster. Thank You for life, for the freedom to live for His glory. We crown Him as Lord of all, and we stand in allegiance to His great name, the name of Christ, in whose name we pray. Amen.

3. As told by Paul Lee Tan, *Encyclopedia of 7,700 Illustrations* (Rockville, Md.: Assurance Publishers, 1979), p. 1231.

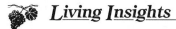

The gnarled olive trees that witnessed that ominous night in the Garden of Gethsemane saw the most treacherous of betrayals—the betrayal of a friend. With a kiss, Judas betrayed the Lord Jesus. In Proverbs 27:6, Solomon said, "Faithful are the wounds of a friend, But deceitful are the kisses of an enemy." And no kiss in the history of the world was more deceitful than the one Judas used to identify Christ to His captors.

If you've ever been betrayed by someone, you know how painful it feels. If that someone was a friend, the hurt is compounded even more.

Can you think back on a time when you felt betrayed? Describe the incident.

_____

_____

_____

_____

_____

Did that experience draw you closer to God, or did it become a source of bitterness that squeezed the life out of your relationship with Him?

_____

Look up the following verses, and describe how they can apply to that situation and to your relationship with the Lord.

Philippians 3:10 _____

_____

1 Corinthians 13:4–5 _____

_____

Ephesians 4:31–32 _____

_____

1 Peter 2:18–23 _____

_____

1 Peter 3:9 _____

_____

2 Corinthians 4:8–10 _____

_____

Possibly, you've not yet forgiven the person who betrayed you. Isn't it time you did? That's the only way you'll be released from the bitterness that binds you. If you have some unfinished business in that area, won't you take a few minutes to bring it before God?

Living Insights
STUDY TWO

Let's spend a few minutes answering some of the questions we raised in today's study. Think back over this past year and reflect on some of the Gethsemane experiences you've encountered.

- Describe a time when you were hailed one day and crucified the next.

_____

_____

_____

_____

_____

- Describe a sleepless night you spent struggling with God's will.

_____

_____

_____

_____

_____

- Describe an experience where you felt so alone you felt like dying.

_____

_____

_____

_____

_____

In your rejection, in your uncertainty, in your aloneness, remember that Jesus has been there too.

> In the days of His flesh, He offered up both prayers and supplications with loud crying and tears to the One able to save Him from death, and He was heard because of His piety. Although He was a Son, He learned obedience from the things which He suffered. (Heb. 5:7–8)

BOOKS FOR
PROBING FURTHER

In this study guide we have examined a number of questions Jesus asked while on earth. These questions forged hooks in people's hearts that tugged at some important issues—issues like personal rivalries, self-sacrifice, and faith. As we examined these issues, we found answers that are as applicable today as they were two thousand years ago.

We hope that the questions not only challenged you but drew you closer to the One who asked them. To further encourage your quest to more intimately know the Savior, we have listed a few books for the journey.

Bruce, A. B. *The Training of the Twelve.* 1894. Reprint. Grand Rapids, Mich.: Kregel Publications, 1971. In this monumental classic, the author deals exhaustively and analytically with the lessons the disciples learned from the Master.

Bruce, F. F. *The Hard Sayings of Jesus.* Downers Grove, Ill.: InterVarsity Press, 1983. The author catalogs seventy difficult statements that Jesus made, and with deft scholarship but down-to-earth simplicity, he explains the cultural and historical context of Jesus' words in order to clarify His message.

Buchanan, Duncan. *The Counselling of Jesus.* Downers Grove, Ill.: InterVarsity Press, 1985. Whether it was Nicodemus at night or the woman at the well at noon, Jesus met people where they were. From there, He extended a hand to help get them on their feet and pointed the way to the gates of His kingdom. The author reviews these life-changing encounters through the eyes of a counselor, and in doing so, he helps create a Christian model for counseling.

Crabb, Larry. *Understanding People.* Grand Rapids, Mich.: Zondervan Publishing House, Ministry Resources Library, 1987. More than any other person who has walked the earth, Jesus understood people; that's why He was such an effective counselor. In this Gold Medallion book, the author—a renowned counselor himself —helps us to sensitively and insightfully understand people so that our words might be better chosen and have a greater impact on their lives.

Lucado, Max. *Six Hours One Friday.* Portland, Oreg.: Multnomah Press, 1989. Several of our lessons dealt with the Passion of our Lord that last week He was on the earth. In this excellent devotional book, the author takes us to the Cross, where we come away with applications that will bring healing to our hurts and rest for our weary hearts.

McDowell, Josh, and Don Stewart. *Answers to Tough Questions Skeptics Ask about the Christian Faith.* San Bernardino, Calif.: Here's Life Publishers, 1980. Jesus asked some tough questions of His critics, but in this book, the roles are reversed. Here the critics get a chance to ask tough questions about Christ and the Christian faith. With skill and scholarship, the authors adroitly field questions that range from "Did Jesus claim to be God?" to "How do we know Jesus rose from the dead?"

Stott, John R. W. *Basic Christianity.* 2d ed. London, England: Inter-Varsity Press, 1971. Reprint. Grand Rapids, Mich.: William B. Eerdmans Publishing Co., 1989. This is an intellectually satisfying book that gives a clear and compelling presentation of the fundamentals of the Christian faith. It deals with the person of Christ, man's need for Christ, Christ's work, and man's response.

Unger, Merrill F. *Demons in the World Today.* Wheaton, Ill.: Tyndale House Publishers, 1971. The author gives a thorough examination of the mysteries of the occult world. If our lesson on the demoniac raised some questions in your mind, here is a good place to go to find biblical answers.

Yancey, Philip. *I Was Just Wondering.* Grand Rapids, Mich.: William B. Eerdmans Publishing Co., 1989. Award-winning author Philip Yancey throws a few questions our way in this probing book. He lures us into the world of provocative insights with a potpourri of subjects that include literature, religion, psychology, and history.

————. *Where Is God When It Hurts?* Grand Rapids, Mich.: Zondervan Publishing House, 1977. When Jesus asked the Father to take the cup from Him that night in Gethsemane, He wrestled with the problem of pain and personal suffering. With refreshing candor, the author asks a question we all ask from time to time— Where is God when it hurts? And he answers it with uncommon scholarship and insight.

NOTES

NOTES

NOTES

NOTES

Insight for Living
Cassette Tapes
ISSUES AND ANSWERS IN JESUS' DAY

You don't have to study Jesus Christ's life very long to realize that He had a remarkably uncomplicated way of getting people to focus on the important issues of life. He simply asked questions. But oh, what amazing questions He asked! And if the answers were slow in coming, what a poignant way He had of bringing the crux of an issue to light.

Another undeniable characteristic of Jesus' teachings is that they were not intended just for the people within earshot. When you read His counsel, you cannot ignore its relevance to the issues we face today. Here is a study that will make you aware that the Scriptures are not only timely, but trustworthy as well.

			U.S.	Canada
IAJ	CS	Cassette series—includes album cover ..	$50.25	$63.75
		Individual cassettes—include messages		
		A and B	5.00	6.35

These prices are subject to change without notice.

IAJ	1-A:	*Who Do People Say the Son of Man Is?*—Matthew 16:13–17
	B:	*What Then Shall I Do with Jesus?*—Matthew 27:11–22
IAJ	2-A:	*Why Do You Seek the Living One among the Dead?*—Luke 24:1–9
	B:	*Did No One Condemn You?*—John 8:1–11
IAJ	3-A:	*Who Is the Greatest in the Kingdom of Heaven?*—Matthew 18:1–6, 10
	B:	*Why Are You So Timid?*—Mark 4:35–41
IAJ	4-A:	*What Is Your Name?*—Mark 5:1–20
	B:	*What Do You See?*—Mark 8:22–26
IAJ	5-A:	*What Do I Have to Do with You?*—John 2:1–11
	B:	*Why Are You Reasoning in Your Hearts?*—Mark 2:1–12
IAJ	6-A:	*What Is That to You?*—John 21:15–22
	B:	*Are You the Teacher . . . and Do Not Understand?*—John 3:1–18
IAJ	7-A:	*The Cup Which the Father Has Given . . . Shall I Not Drink It?*—John 18:1–11
	B:	*How Long Has This Been Happening?*—Mark 9:14–29
IAJ	8-A:	*Do You Know What I Have Done?*—John 13:1–17
	B:	*Shall Not God Bring About Justice?*—Luke 18:1–8
IAJ	9-A:	*Why Do You Stand Looking into the Sky?*—Acts 1:1–11
	B:	*Sharing the Meaning of Life**—Matthew 26:36–50, 28:1–8

* This message was not a part of the original series but is compatible with it.

How to Order by Mail

Simply mark on the order form whether you want the series or individual tapes. Mail the form with your payment to the appropriate address listed below. We will process your order as promptly as we can.

United States: Mail your order to the Sales Department at Insight for Living, Post Office Box 4444, Fullerton, California 92634. If you wish your order to be shipped first-class for faster delivery, add 10 percent of the total order amount (not including California sales tax). Otherwise, please allow four to six weeks for delivery by fourth-class mail. We accept personal checks, money orders, Visa, or Master-Card in payment for materials. Unfortunately, we are unable to offer invoicing or COD orders.

Canada: Mail your order to Insight for Living Ministries, Post Office Box 2510, Vancouver, British Columbia V6B 3W7. Please add 7 percent of your total order for first-class postage and allow approximately four weeks for delivery. Our listeners in British Columbia must also add a 6 percent sales tax to the total of all tape orders (not including postage). We accept personal checks, money orders, Visa, or MasterCard in payment for materials. Unfortunately, we are unable to offer invoicing or COD orders.

Australia, New Zealand, or Papua New Guinea: Mail your order to Insight for Living, Inc., GPO Box 2823 EE, Melbourne, Victoria 3001, Australia. Please allow six to ten weeks for delivery by surface mail. If you would like your order sent airmail, the delivery time may be reduced. Whether you choose surface or airmail, postage costs must be added to the amount of purchase and included with your order. Please use the chart that follows to determine correct postage. Due to fluctuating currency rates, we can accept only personal checks made payable in U.S. funds, international money orders, Visa, or MasterCard in payment for materials.

Overseas: Other overseas residents should contact our United States office. Please allow six to ten weeks for delivery by surface mail. If you would like your order sent airmail, the delivery time may be reduced. Whether you choose surface or airmail, postage costs must be added to the amount of purchase and included with your order. Please use the chart that follows to determine correct postage. Due to fluctuating currency rates, we can accept only personal checks made payable in U.S. funds, international money orders, Visa, or MasterCard in payment for materials.

Type of Postage	Postage Cost
Surface	10% of total order
Airmail	25% of total order

For Faster Service, Order by Telephone

To purchase using Visa or MasterCard, you are welcome to use our **toll-free** numbers between the hours of 8:30 A.M. and 4:00 P.M., Pacific time, Monday through Friday. The number to call from anywhere in the United States is **1-800-772-8888.** To order from Canada, call our Vancouver office at **1-800-663-7639.** Vancouver residents should call (604) 272-5811. Telephone orders from overseas are handled through our Sales Department at (714) 870-9161. We are unable to accept collect calls.

Our Guarantee

Our cassettes are guaranteed for ninety days against faulty performance or breakage due to a defect in the tape. For best results, please be sure your tape recorder is in good operating condition and is cleaned regularly.

Note: To cover processing and handling, there is a $10 fee for *any* returned check.

Order Form

IAJ CS represents the entire *Issues and Answers in Jesus' Day* series, while IAJ 1–9 are the individual tapes included in the series.

Series or Tape	Unit Price U.S.	Canada	Quantity	Amount
IAJ CS	$50.25	$63.75		$
IAJ 1	5.00	6.35		
IAJ 2	5.00	6.35		
IAJ 3	5.00	6.35		
IAJ 4	5.00	6.35		
IAJ 5	5.00	6.35		
IAJ 6	5.00	6.35		
IAJ 7	5.00	6.35		
IAJ 8	5.00	6.35		
IAJ 9	5.00	6.35		
			Subtotal	
		Sales Tax 6¼% for orders delivered in California; 6% in British Columbia.		
		Postage 7% in Canada; overseas residents, see "How to Order by Mail."		
	10% Optional First-Class Shipping and Handling United States residents only.			
	Gift to Insight for Living Tax-deductible in the United States and Canada.			
		Total Amount Due Please do not send cash.	$	

If there is a balance: ☐ apply it as a donation ☐ please refund

Form of payment:

☐ Check or money order made payable to Insight for Living
☐ Credit card (circle one): Visa MasterCard
  Card Number _____ Expiration Date _____
  Signature _____
  We cannot process your credit card purchase without your signature.

Name _____

Address _____

City _____

State/Province_____ Zip/Postal Code _____

Country _____

Telephone (   ) _____ Radio Station ___ ___ ___ ___
  If questions arise concerning your order, we may need to contact you.

Mail this order form to the Sales Department at one of these addresses:
Insight for Living, Post Office Box 4444, Fullerton, CA 92634
Insight for Living Ministries, Post Office Box 2510, Vancouver, BC, Canada V6B 3W7
Insight for Living, Inc., GPO Box 2823 EE, Melbourne, VIC 3001, Australia

Order Form

IAJ CS represents the entire *Issues and Answers in Jesus' Day* series, while IAJ 1–9 are the individual tapes included in the series.

Series or Tape	Unit Price U.S.	Canada	Quantity	Amount
IAJ CS	$50.25	$63.75		$
IAJ 1	5.00	6.35		
IAJ 2	5.00	6.35		
IAJ 3	5.00	6.35		
IAJ 4	5.00	6.35		
IAJ 5	5.00	6.35		
IAJ 6	5.00	6.35		
IAJ 7	5.00	6.35		
IAJ 8	5.00	6.35		
IAJ 9	5.00	6.35		
			Subtotal	
			Sales Tax 6¼% *for orders delivered in California; 6% in British Columbia.*	
			Postage 7% *in Canada; overseas residents, see "How to Order by Mail."*	
			10% Optional First-Class Shipping and Handling *United States residents only.*	
			Gift to Insight for Living *Tax-deductible in the United States and Canada.*	
			Total Amount Due *Please do not send cash.*	$

If there is a balance: ☐ apply it as a donation ☐ please refund

Form of payment:

☐ Check or money order made payable to Insight for Living

☐ Credit card (circle one): Visa MasterCard

Card Number _____ Expiration Date _____

Signature _____
We cannot process your credit card purchase without your signature.

Name _____

Address _____

City _____

State/Province_____ Zip/Postal Code _____

Country _____

Telephone _(___)_____ Radio Station ___ ___ ___ ___
If questions arise concerning your order, we may need to contact you.

Mail this order form to the Sales Department at one of these addresses:
Insight for Living, Post Office Box 4444, Fullerton, CA 92634
Insight for Living Ministries, Post Office Box 2510, Vancouver, BC, Canada V6B 3W7
Insight for Living, Inc., GPO Box 2823 EE, Melbourne, VIC 3001, Australia

Order Form

IAJ CS represents the entire *Issues and Answers in Jesus' Day* series, while IAJ 1–9 are the individual tapes included in the series.

Series or Tape	Unit Price U.S.	Canada	Quantity	Amount
IAJ CS	$50.25	$63.75		$
IAJ 1	5.00	6.35		
IAJ 2	5.00	6.35		
IAJ 3	5.00	6.35		
IAJ 4	5.00	6.35		
IAJ 5	5.00	6.35		
IAJ 6	5.00	6.35		
IAJ 7	5.00	6.35		
IAJ 8	5.00	6.35		
IAJ 9	5.00	6.35		
			Subtotal	
			Sales Tax 6¼% for orders delivered in California; 6% in British Columbia.	
			Postage 7% in Canada; overseas residents, see "How to Order by Mail."	
			10% Optional First-Class Shipping and Handling United States residents only.	
			Gift to Insight for Living Tax-deductible in the United States and Canada.	
			Total Amount Due Please do not send cash.	$

If there is a balance: ☐ apply it as a donation ☐ please refund

Form of payment:

☐ Check or money order made payable to Insight for Living

☐ Credit card (circle one):   Visa   MasterCard

Card Number _____ Expiration Date _____

Signature _____
We cannot process your credit card purchase without your signature.

Name _____

Address _____

City _____

State/Province_____ Zip/Postal Code _____

Country _____

Telephone (____)_____ Radio Station ___ ___ ___ ___
If questions arise concerning your order, we may need to contact you.

Mail this order form to the Sales Department at one of these addresses:
Insight for Living, Post Office Box 4444, Fullerton, CA 92634
Insight for Living Ministries, Post Office Box 2510, Vancouver, BC, Canada V6B 3W7
Insight for Living, Inc., GPO Box 2823 EE, Melbourne, VIC 3001, Australia